TEACHING
LARGE
CLASSES

SURVIVAL SKILLS FOR SCHOLARS

Managing Editor: Peter Labella

Survival Skills for Scholars provides you, the professor or advanced graduate student working in a college or university setting, with practical suggestions for making the most of your academic career. These brief, readable guides will help you with skills that you are required to master as a college professor but may have never been taught in graduate school. Using hands-on, jargon-free advice and examples, forms, lists, and suggestions for additional resources, experts on different aspects of academic life give invaluable tips on managing the day-to-day tasks of academia—effectively and efficiently.

Volumes in This Series

SURVIVAL SKILLS FOR SCHOLARS

TEACHING LARGE CLASSES

Tools and Strategies

ELISA CARBONE

SAGE Publications
International Educational and Professional Publisher
Thousand Oaks   London   New Delhi

For information:

SAGE Publications, Inc.
2455 Teller Road
Thousand Oaks, California 91320
E-mail@sagepub.com

SAGE Publications Ltd.
6 Bonhill Street
London EC2A 4PU
United Kingdom

SAGE Publications India Pvt. Ltd.
M-32 Market
Greater Kailash I
New Delhi 110048 India

Printed in the United States of America

Library of Congress Cataloging-in-Publication Data

Carbone, Elisa Lynn.
  Teaching large classes : tools and strategies / by Elisa
Carbone.
    p. cm. — (Survival skills for scholars ; v. 19)
  Includes bibliographical references and index.
  ISBN 0-7619-0974-5 (cloth : acid-free paper)
  ISBN 0-7619-0975-3 (pbk. : acid-free paper)
  1. College teaching—United States. 2. Class size—United States.
3. Lecture method in teaching. I. Title. II. Series.
  LB2331 .C336 1998
  378.12—ddc21
                                                    98-19671

98 99 00 01 02 03 04 8 7 6 5 4 3 2 1

Acquiring Editor:	Peter Labella
Editorial Assistant:	Corrine Pierce
Production Editor:	Michele Lingre
Editorial Assistant:	Denise Santoyo
Designer/Typesetter:	Danielle Dillahunt
Cover Designer:	Candice Harman
Print Buyer	Anna Chin

Contents

II. PRESENTING THE MATERIAL

III. GETTING YOUR STUDENTS INVOLVED

IV. MANAGING YOUR LARGE CLASS

Foreword

Large classes present a special challenge for institutions of higher education and those of us who teach in them—a particular challenge that is not present in K-12 classrooms, where the majority of teaching and learning challenges have been studied most deeply.

At a time when much has been discerned—and discussed—about the importance of active learning, student-centered teaching, and shared responsibility for the success of student-learning outcomes, large classes (in our definition, over 100 students) represent an anomaly. How can you personalize your teaching and make it more interactive when you have so many students to deal with? This question, asked many times—and repeatedly—by a growing number of college professors, poses the dilemma that this book attempts to ameliorate. By answering the question directly, and taking its referent seriously and realistically, the chapters in this book offer tangible assistance and potential relief.

Although it might be ideal to be able to change all the large classes into small ones, that's just not going to happen. The economic and traditional realities that control most decisions at colleges and universities won't allow it. The alternative is to support a serious attempt to improve the situation within the realistic and comprehensive context of priorities that we face in higher education. That's how this project began.

The "Large Classes Project" arose out of a University of Maryland campuswide engagement with Continuous Quality Improvement (CQI, aka TQM, Total Quality Management). As part of a major commitment to use the processes of CQI to improve important aspects of the university environment, each campus vice president was asked to choose a significant issue to tackle through a dedicated CQI project designed to identify underlying problems and propose solutions. The Vice President for Academic Affairs selected the issue of large classes as the priority concern for this extraordinary initiative.

It's important that this topic was identified as a priority issue by the top level of our campus academic administration. By doing so, the institution officially recognized that the matter of improving large classes exists in a context—indeed in a kind of ecological system—consisting of theoretical frameworks for teaching and learning, administrative structures and customary procedures for decision making (Who teaches these classes? What criteria? What supports will be given?), limitations of physical facilities, and instructor skill and effectiveness levels. Consistent with this recognition, the CQI Large Classes Team was assembled with attention to the "cross-functional" nature of the problem to be addressed. Faculty from many disciplines; administrators from the domains of student services, facilities, and finance; and students from graduate and undergraduate levels were included in the team. Because the Center for Teaching Excellence, located in the office of the Dean for Undergraduate Studies, was a logical place to assume central leadership on this issue, I was asked to chair the team.

With the help of a professional facilitator who possessed expertise in CQI processes, the Large Classes Team established a schedule of weekly meetings and began to attack the problem by brainstorming what the underlying problems might be, what data we needed to inform our work, and how we could best respond to this daunting challenge on a university campus with hundreds of classes in the "large" category, 35,000 students, and 3,000 faculty members—most of whom had little if any education in the area of pedagogy. We succeeded in designing and implementing a very effective process, which included gathering systematic data from faculty who taught large classes, students who had experience in taking large classes, and some administrators who had access to additional relevant data. The team produced a number of data-based recommendations, and these recommendations reflected our strong sense that responsibility for improving large classes needed to be taken by the faculty who taught these classes, of course, but also by the departments, colleges, and central administrative offices whose decisions have such a great impact on these faculty. Recommendations included the need for self-studies of selection and reward system procedures (we found a tremendous variation here) used by departments and colleges in administering large classes, facilities rehabilitation, and an array of faculty development initiatives that could stimulate individual creative solutions within the discipline, build on some good examples and practices already present on campus, and support accessible and practical assistance for the many faculty and teaching assistants called upon to teach undergraduates in these large class environments. The Center for Teaching Excellence (CTE) was asked to coordinate a number of these improvement efforts. Among the first recommendations we responded to was the creation of a *Large Classes Handbook* (written by Dr. Jennifer Robinson, then a member of the CTE staff), which was mailed to every faculty member identified as teaching a class of 100 students or more. This initial effort was well received and set the stage for more extensive activities.

With the support of Robert Hampton, Associate Provost and Dean for Undergraduate Studies, we were able to attract Elisa Carbone to join the CTE and serve as coordinator of the "Large Classes Project." Elisa's experience in teaching and in other aspects of faculty development, with an emphasis on effective lecturing skills, provided just the right resources for this project, and her personal vitality and ability to communicate so well made her involvement a very happy piece of this endeavor. Elisa and I examined the scope of the large classes issue, diagrammed various possibilities, and analyzed what had been done and what might be most fruitful to do as a next step; and then Elisa came up with a stupendous idea, the *Large Classes Newsletter*, an idea that became the basis for the contents of this book. By combining research on the successful strategies, good ideas, and experienced insights of a variety of faculty; by visiting classes and observing effective techniques in action; and by sampling relevant professional literature in the field, Elisa could gather truly useful and original content to communicate to interested faculty. Indeed, that's what she has done, and we are delighted that readers from many other campuses now will be able to share some of the fine ideas that have emerged from this project.

Taken together, this compilation is a valuable asset. It is an individual creative achievement for Elisa Carbone and a contribution of a University of Maryland process that has effectively combined top-level support from Academic Affairs and Undergraduate Studies with institutional coordination by the Center for Teaching Excellence and Elisa's talent and hard work. The ideas and suggestions should relate well to all teachers and institutions seeking solutions for the tough problem of improving large classes and making learning in *all* environments a productive, enjoyable, and positive experience—both for their students and for themselves.

—*Jim Greenberg*

Acknowledgments

I would like to thank:

Jim Greenberg, Director of the Center for Teaching Excellence, who got me started in the Large Classes Project and supported me every step of the way.

Robert Hampton, Associate Provost and Dean for Undergraduate Studies, for his leadership, commitment to the Project, and ongoing financial support.

Marianne Eismann, Assistant to the Dean, for her expert editing of my first drafts, and all of the faculty members who welcomed me into classrooms and offices to share their teaching expertise.

Introduction

Listening to the Experts

In the fall of 1995 I was invited to work with Jim Greenberg on the "Large Classes Project" at the Center For Teaching Excellence (CTE) at the University of Maryland College Park (UMCP). We had a small budget and a large goal: help our faculty to improve their teaching in large classes.

First, I had to be brought-up-to-date, because the work had begun the year before. I studied the results of student and faculty questionnaires and focus groups, read materials that had been developed, such as the *Large Classes Handbook*, visited classrooms where large classes were being taught, and met with Jim and several faculty members who had been involved in the previous discussions of this issue.

Next, Jim and I dove into brainstorming. We took out a large sheet of newsprint and several colored markers (essential equipment for deep thought) and started throwing around possibilities. We wanted something that would reach as many faculty as possible and be as effective as possible. Individual meetings with faculty often seemed to have the greatest impact on teaching improvement, but it would not be practical to meet with each large class instructor. So, whereas individual meetings wouldn't work as a way to reach everyone, we decided to keep them in mind because of their effectiveness. In addition, the CTE already had an excellent seminar series under way and the feedback from these sessions had been quite positive. We could plan workshops aimed specifically toward large classes faculty, but we knew that only a fraction of the 300 of them would attend. Some faculty weren't *asking* for new teaching ideas, so we needed something to get them interested in a way that faculty workshops didn't always do. We decided to keep faculty seminars on our list of options, with the recognition that they would not be the total answer. We left that afternoon with a very colorful piece of newsprint, and no definitive decisions about what to do next.

New ideas tend to ripen with age. During the next several weeks a plan began to take shape. Individual meetings with faculty could be used to "pick their brains" for what was working well in their classrooms. This would show recognition and value for their good practices. This information then could be shared in a series of articles in a newsletter. Large classes faculty would receive, every month or so, ideas from their peers. Then, in the privacy of their own offices, they could make decisions about whether or not their own teaching practices could use a little infusion of new strategies from the newsletter. It would be like a faculty workshop by mail. The newsletter would be interesting (I even hired a cartoonist!), would reach everyone, and would show appreciation for the talent present at UMCP. The *Large Classes Newsletter* was born.

The information for the newsletter has been gleaned by listening to the experts. They are not necessarily the most published faculty, nor are they all nationally known leaders of seminars on large classes teaching. They are the instructors who, for years, have been teaching large classes, learning by trial and error, coming up with terrific ideas, and quietly using them semester after semester in their own classes. I added to their input some of the excellent information I found in the literature about each topic.

Here is how we got the newsletter started: First, we sent out a questionnaire and a plea for help. "We're planning a *Large Classes Newsletter*," we said, "and we'd like to know who is good at using active learning in large classes, who makes their classes personal, who has good ideas for the first class of the semester," and so forth. There were 11 topics, and a space under each one for faculty to fill in their own name or the name of a colleague whom they knew to be successfully using some teaching idea. The topics were derived from the concerns we'd been hearing from both students and faculty in the brainstorming sessions and questionnaire research that preceded this stage of the project. From the list of topics and faculty responses, I compiled a list of names from which to begin the research.

For some topics, I invited faculty to attend a brainstorming session. Over grapes and cheese we discussed the issue. Ideas built on other ideas and I took notes on pitfalls and suggestions. For other topics, I visited classrooms and conducted face-to-face or phone interviews. As I went along, the original list of faculty to contact kept growing. I'd call someone about, say, lecturing tips. He or she would volunteer to let me visit the class, and also add that so-and-so had some great ideas about lecturing as well. Or I'd call to invite someone to the brainstorming session on classroom management. After agreeing to come, he or she would add, "I heard that Mady Segal's students don't come in late *or* leave early. Could you please find out how in the world she does that?" or "Someone told me Howard Smead from History has a fool-proof method of taking attendance in a large lecture hall. You should call him and find out how he does it." And I'd have two more names on my list.

As the research continued, more topics were added. We sent out several more questionnaires asking for more names (there are different faculty teaching large classes each semester, and we didn't want to leave anyone out), and asking "What question would you like to ask other teachers of large classes?" and "What topic are you interested in that we haven't covered yet?"

The response has been excellent. We have letters to the editor, requests for copies of the newsletter from faculty who want to pass them on to their teaching assistants (TAs), letters from faculty thanking me for reporting so well on their teaching practices, and always another volunteer saying "you can visit my class." Faculty tell us it's helpful to see what others are doing, and that they appreciate the fact that *specific* strategies are presented. As one instructor wrote, "[The Newsletter] always has a tip or idea. When I try them, they *work!*"

Two and a half years of the newsletter, with information added when my editor at Sage, Peter Labella, felt it would be helpful, have become this book. I hope that it will be as valuable to you in your teaching of large classes as it has been to the faculty I've worked with to put it together.

STARTING OUT RIGHT

1 | Starting the Semester

The First Class

You've been scheduled to teach a large lecture class MWF at 10:00 A.M. Do one or more of these dreams crop up for you before the first day of the semester?

> Dream #1: On the morning of your first class you oversleep, get stuck in traffic, and can't find your room. You arrive 45 minutes late and all of your students have left.
>
> Dream #2: You forget all about the class until 9:30 A.M., whereupon you drive to campus like a maniac and arrive only 10 minutes late. All of your students are still there, but when you step up to the lectern you realize that you haven't prepared a lecture. In fact, you don't even know the title of the course.
>
> Dream #3: You awaken early feeling rested. You have a relaxing drive to campus and get a good parking space. You arrive in your classroom with copious lecture notes, on time . . . in your pajamas.

If any of these dreams plague your sleep during the last few weeks before the start of the semester, you may well be suffering from a case of "first-class" anxiety (or is it a first class case of anxiety?) The suggestions in this chapter are designed to restore peaceful slumber.

3

First Impressions

First impressions *do* count. During the first class meeting, the example you set for things like promptness, interest level of course material, and student involvement will create expectations that will last the entire semester. Although there may be rare occasions when you can't avoid being late, don't let the first day of class be one of them. If you'd like to give the class an informal, personal feel, plan to arrive a few minutes early and chat with students as they arrive. If you're the more formal sort, make your entrance a minute or so before the start of class and launch right into your content.

If you simply go over the syllabus and other administrative matters and then dismiss students, you will have made the session *brief* and *boring*. This will have set the tone for the rest of the semester. Do go over the syllabus but then use the rest of the time to stimulate students' interest in your subject matter. As J. Richard Aronson (1987) suggests, "Be a missionary. . . . Explain why understanding your subject is essential for lifelong happiness and fulfillment; why without your course one cannot be an interesting or attractive person. Whet their appetites for what is to come" (p. 32).

Kris Dhawale (1994) suggests using a lecture and demonstration as a way to spark students' interest. In the first session of her introductory chemistry class, she "converts" copper into silver and then into gold. She does this by heating zinc powder and 10% sodium hydroxide solution and placing a piece of copper wire into it. The wire turns a silvery white. Then, she washes the wire and heats it in a flame. It transforms to a golden color. She invites students to wonder, Is it real? Is it magic? Is it science? She finds that the mystery, along with the visual elements of the demonstration, creates a thought-provoking basis from which to discuss science and scientific methods. Only after this awakening experience does she delve into the syllabus.

Getting students involved is another way to spark their interest. Individually, with the person next to them, or in groups of three or four (just have them twist around in those bolted-down chairs to form these groups), invite them to do some brainstorming about the course. Here are some possible questions to pose.

- What have you heard about the course?
- What do you already know about the content?
- What would you like to gain from the course (besides credit)?
- What are your goals for this course?

A few students then may be asked to share with the whole class several of the responses that emerged in their groups. Not everyone will have a chance to participate in this whole-class discussion, but everyone will have participated in their small groups. It is also of interest to invite students to save their answers to these questions. Later in the semester they can look back at their answers and see how far they've come toward reaching their goals and adding to their knowledge of the course material.

The Syllabus

One way to help students lay claim to the work laid out for them in the syllabus is to provide a space in which they should fill in their name. It's a small step that says, "Responsibility for the reading, homework, and tests required by this syllabus is *mine.*" You also may want to provide a space on the syllabus where they can record their answers to the above questions (Hamilton, 1994). That way, when it is time to review their answers later in the semester, they won't have disappeared into the ethers.

A high percentage of students in large classes are freshmen and sophomores. It can be very helpful to them to include a section in your syllabus titled "How to Succeed in This Class." Be specific about how much time they should invest in the course, how important attendance will be for their grade, how to approach homework assignments, how to work for under-standing, and how to study for exams.

Breaking the Ice

The logistics in a large class don't lend themselves to those wonderful icebreakers that are available for small classes. For example, it is not practical for each student to introduce a partner to the rest of the class. There are, however, ways to help students get a sense of whom they are taking this class with. Wilbert McKeachie (1994) suggests asking for a show of hands to indicate how many freshmen, sophomores, juniors, seniors, and/or out-of-state students there are in the lecture hall. This gives students a sense of the makeup of the class and how they fit in.

Robyn Muncy (History) uses this technique on the first day of class and also poses a few questions whose answers will be helpful to her in planning the content of her lectures. She asks about what movies and television shows her students are familiar with. "How many of you have seen the movie *Scream*? How about *Secrets and Lies*? For how many of you is your favorite TV show *Murphy Brown*? Whose favorite is *Roseanne*?" Answers to questions such as these let her know, for example, what types of female role models her students are tuned-in to. The more she knows about her students' attitudes, the more effectively she can gear her lectures to reach them.

It is also helpful to have students turn to the person next to them on the first day, introduce themselves, and trade phone numbers. That way, they immediately know at least one other person in the class, and they have someone to call in case they must miss a lecture.

First-Class Anxiety

Fear of speaking to a large group is natural, but rather than let nervousness get to you, try using it to your advantage. Many performers see the "butterflies" as energy and use them to pump dynamism into their presentation. Or try a method I learned from a well-known public speaker: Fool yourself. Tell yourself that the arousal of the autonomic nervous system you are experiencing—sweaty palms, increased heart rate, fluttery stomach—is *not* fear but anticipation, enthusiasm, and excitement about that first day of class!

References

Aronson, R. J. (1987). Six keys to effective instruction in large classes: Advice from a practitioner. In M. Weimer (Ed.), *New directions for teaching and learning: Teaching large classes well* (pp. 31-37). San Francisco: Jossey-Bass.

Dhawale, K. (1994). Ice breaking demo. In E. Bender, M. Dunn, B. Kendall, C. Larson, & P. Wilkes (Eds.). *Quick hits: Successful strategies by award winning teachers* (p. 2). Bloomington: Indiana University Press.

Hamilton, S. (1994). Their goals first. In E. Bender, M. Dunn, B. Kendall, C. Larson, & P. Wilkes (Eds.), *Quick hits: Successful strategies by award winning teachers* (P.6). Bloomington, Indiana University Press.

McKeachie, W. J. (1994). *Teaching tips: Strategies, research, and theory for college and university teachers* (9th ed.). Lexington, MA: D.C. Heath.

2 | Personalizing the Large Class

He's gone from sharing a bedroom with his kid brother to bunking in with a stranger from New Jersey. She's gone from fighting over the shower with her two sisters to sharing a bathroom with the whole east wing of the girls' dorm. They used to be known by their first names, now they're identified by social security numbers. And after 12 years of classes with 30 or so students, they find themselves in a lecture hall with 300 other freshmen.

One of the biggest problems with large classes, students report, is that the impersonal atmosphere makes them feel anonymous, lost, and out of place, and these feelings lead to decreased motivation (Ward & Jenkins, 1992; Wulff, Nyquist, & Abbott, 1987). Is there anything we can do to help students in large classes feel more welcome? Below you'll find some effective and efficient ways to make large classes more personal.

Act as if the Class Were Small

Maryellen Gleason (1986) advises teachers of large classes to use some of the same communication behaviors as do teachers of small classes. Come in early and chat informally with a few students. Move around the room as you lecture. When a student asks a question, move closer to that student as you answer the question. Join teaching assistants in distributing handouts. Stay after class to briefly discuss the lecture and answer questions for students who are interested. Rather than allow the podium to separate you from your class, engage the students in the same way you would students in your small classes. This can do a lot to show students that you are interested in them and you are accessible.

Learn Student Names

Learn the names of hundreds of students? It may seem impossible, but many large-classes faculty members work toward that goal. Robyn Muncy (History) has her students state their name each time they ask a question. This helps her remember at least some of their names and lets all of her students know that she is trying to learn them. "The effort is more important than complete success," she says. "If students see you making an effort to get to know them, they feel you care and that it's worth coming to see you during your office hours."

Mady Segal (Sociology) *does* strive for complete success in learning the names of all 140 of her students. On the first day of the semester, her teaching assistants (TAs) get busy lining up students in groups of three or four and snapping a Polaroid picture of them. They write students' names under their photos and staple them onto an index card. This is when Segal's work begins. During "down time," such as sitting at stop lights or walking from her car to her office, she studies the names and faces and memorizes them as one would memorize elements on the periodic table. Within a few weeks she knows all of her students by name.

In order to continue to remember these many names, it is helpful to use them constantly, every time you go to class, every time you see the students around campus. What if a student drops the class? Simply put an X through the photo. Segal finds that often by the time a student drops, she has already committed the name to memory. Then, when she sees the student walking down Campus Drive she can stop him and ask, "So, Bill, why did you drop my class?"

Segal finds that learning their names greatly increases the rapport she has with her students. They really appreciate having an instructor who takes the time to learn who they are. With the increasing number of international students in today's classrooms, learning names often includes learning pronunciations. "It becomes painfully obvious when you blatantly avoid speaking to a student with a foreign-sounding name," says Uma Krishnaswami of the Department of Special Education. She suggests writing down unfamiliar names phonetically, practicing them, and asking students to confirm that your pronunciations are correct. "People feel respected when you make an effort to say their names right," says Krishnaswami.

Personalize Feedback

"No aspect of the large class is as demanding of instructors' time or as likely to pressure them to adopt impersonal evaluation methods as are the challenges of grading and giving feedback" (Lowman, 1987, p. 78). What are some practical ways to personalize feedback in large classes? Gleason (1986) suggested choosing 20 papers each time an exam or assignment is given and adding a few personal comments. In this way, by the end of the semester you probably will have given feedback to a fairly large portion of the class. Or, have TAs select the highest-scoring papers for you to write comments on. This "reward" can add to students' motivation.

The "one-minute paper" can be a very valuable tool to create a kind of dialogue with students. Ask them to take out a sheet of paper, at the end of class, and give some kind of input about the class. This may be to write one or two main points they heard in the lecture, jot down one area they're still confused about, or to pose a question they have about the topic you've been covering. These "papers" will be very brief and will not take a great deal of time to read through. They will make you aware of how well students are following your lecture, let you know if many students share an area of confusion (so you can provide clarification during the next class session), and keep you abreast of students' questions. You may want to choose several questions to answer during the next class session. This will help students know that their individual voices are being heard.

Invite Input From Students

Improved communication always begins with listening. One way to listen to students in a large class is to ask for their input through a brief survey or questionnaire. Good questions to ask might include the following:

- What elements in the class have been most helpful?
- In what areas are you having difficulty?
- What suggestions do you have for ways to improve the class?

Jensen and Robinson (1995) found that simply giving students a chance to offer input seemed to improve their morale.

Another way to use a questionnaire is to gather such personal information as "What activities do you participate in?" This information can be used, anonymously in the form of statistics, to give the class some personality. For example, "We have six members of the lacrosse team, nine members of Phi Eta Sigma Honor Society, 72 members of sororities and fraternities, and three members of the yearbook staff." It helps students feel a sense of identity. Rather than feeling, as one student put it, "like numbers at the end of a computer printout" (Ward & Jenkins, 1992, p. 23), they become a group of *individuals*.

Be Available

Students in large classes don't always feel comfortable coming to office hours. The distance that is created between the podium and the rows of seats makes them feel intimidated by the thought of meeting individually with the professor. Faculty members who plan ways to make themselves more approachable find that this encourages students to attend their office hours and partake of the extra learning that this more personal contact provides.

Penny Koines (Plant Biology) schedules an informal meeting time: a brown-bag lunch in the conference room every Wednesday at noon. Eight or nine students attend each Wednesday session to discuss questions they have about the class material or to talk about environmental issues from the current media. A core of five or six students comes every week, along with a number of students who attend one or two meetings when they have specific questions. Koines has found that even though only a small percentage of the entire class of 250 attends these sessions, the fact that she is available to *eat* with students has made everyone in the class feel that she is more accessible and approachable. The informal lunch meeting, she says, has helped all students feel more comfortable about attending her formal office hours.

Robyn Muncy periodically holds her office hours in the reference section of the library. This way, she can personally show students where to find the materials they need for research for her class. "Only ten students may show up for this," she says, "but that's ten students I wouldn't have reached otherwise."

In classes with large numbers of students, personal contact with each student may well be impossible. But, with some effort, it is possible to help students feel less anonymous and more valued as individuals.

References

Gleason, M. (1986). Better communication in large courses. *College Teaching, 34*(1), 20-24.
Jensen, P. A., & Robinson, J. K. (1995, January). Deming's quality principles applied to a large lecture course. *Journal of Engineering Education, 84*(1), 45-50.

Lowman, J. (1987). Giving students feedback. In M. Weimer (Ed.), *New directions for teaching and learning: Teaching large classes well* (pp. 71-83). San Francisco: Jossey-Bass.

Ward, A., & Jenkins, A. (1992). The problems of learning and teaching in large classes. In G. Gibbs & A. Jenkins (Eds.), *Teaching large classes in higher education* (pp. 23-36). London: Kegan Paul.

Wulff, D. H., Nyquist, J. D., & Abbott, R. D. (1987). Students' perceptions of large classes. In M. Weimer (Ed.), *New directions for teaching and learning: Teaching large classes well* (pp. 17-30). San Francisco: Jossey-Bass.

PRESENTING THE MATERIAL

3 | Lecturing 101:
Getting Your Students to Listen

The spoken word belongs half to him who speaks and half to him who hears.

—French Proverb

Whether your material is five minutes of directions or a three-hour lecture, if your students have tuned you out, the reason can be summed up in two words: internal noise. No, that's not heart palpitations and stomach rumblings. It's the inner dialogue and mental tangents that take students out of the classroom and transport them into their personal daydreams. It's not a malicious thing on their part; they want to listen, they try to listen, but before they know it, in their minds it's Saturday night and the frat party is *cranking!*

Some internal noise is outside the instructor's control: *"I really want to go home this weekend."* or *"I'm worried about my credit card bill."* But some of the distractions in a class begin with a reaction to the method, style, or content of the professor's message: *"This doesn't relate to my life."* *"I'm confused; what's coming next?"* *"This teacher is biased or sexist. He or she can't teach me anything."*

As teachers, our sphere of influence lies in *what* we present and *how* we present it. If we can avoid triggering students' internal noise, we will be helping them to listen more effectively.

Help Students Create Connections

(Internal Noise: *"This doesn't relate to my life."*)

In *From Communication to Curriculum*, Douglas Barnes (1992) writes, "Learning is not just a matter of receiving information; students need to be helped to develop their grasp of new ideas and ways of understanding and to relate them to their existing experience of the world" (p. 5).

Everyone retains information more readily when the purpose of that information is both evident and personal. Helping our students to find connections between the information we present in class and their own needs, goals, and desires, is one of the most valuable things we can do for them. A number of teaching methods, such as reflective journaling, think-pair-share, or a "needs, goals, and objectives" paper at the beginning of the semester, can help students brainstorm about ways in which what they are learning will make their lives richer.

Reflective journaling may be as simple as posting a question or two about course goals on an overhead and providing a period of about five minutes for students to write their responses. These responses may be turned in or kept by students for their personal use. A few minutes of reflection at the beginning of the course can help students become clearer about what they would like to gain from the class and help them to be more committed to attaining those goals.

Think-pair-share is a simple, cooperative learning technique (for more on cooperative learning, see Chapter 6 on active learning) that may be used easily in large classes. First, ask students to *think* about their answer to a question. In this case, the question might be, "What is the most important thing I'd like to gain from this class?" Next, invite students to *pair* with another student and *share* their answers with each other. The sharing may continue by asking a few students to report their answers to the entire group. This method helps students clarify their goals not only through personal reflection but also through brainstorming with another student.

If you would like to be more formal about this early goal setting, a "needs, goals, and objectives" paper may fit the bill. On the first day of class I give my students their first written assignment: First, look over the syllabus, look over the textbook, take account of what we will be covering in this course. Then, make three lists.

1. What do I want or need to learn from this class (be specific— this is a *list*, not a sentence).
2. What are my goals for this course, that is, by the end of the class I want to know or have or be able to do these things, . . . (again, a list).
3. If I reach these goals, how will my life be improved? Consider academics, career, family, and self. List as many areas as possible.

I have found that it is important to require this assignment to be typed. Students definitely put more thought and effort into a paper that must be typed in comparison to one that can be scribbled quickly during the 5 minutes before class starts. These papers are also excellent resources for students to look back at later in the semester to see how far they've come in reaching their goals.

Once students have formulated and shared their goals, especially if you've made them into written assignments and have read them, it is important to *respond* to them. Let students know their voices have been heard and their needs have been taken into consideration. I generally group the most common goals together and tell students how I will be helping them to meet these goals during the semester through the course content and format. If there are areas of content I had planned to gloss over or not spend much time on, yet quite a few students mention these as areas they'd like to improve their skills in or learn more about, then I let them know that I'll be adjusting the course content a bit in order to meet their needs.

When students have a grasp of the purpose of your class in their lives and the purpose of their learning, the listening comes naturally.

Maintain Your Credibility—
Don't Lose Your Listeners Through Self-Deprecation

(Internal Noise: "*This is worthless. I don't have to listen.*")

It's a natural human desire to downplay our performance at any task in the hope that what we present will then exceed people's expectations. For example, "You can come over, but my house is a mess." That way, any straightening that gets done is a plus. If the house is still a mess, they've been warned.

Our classroom presentations can fall prey to this natural human tendency. But, warning our students before a lecture that it may not be perfect, that it may not be vitally important, or that they may have trouble understanding it, creates a self-fulfilling prophecy. Students assume the lecture will be mediocre, unnecessary, and/or over their heads—and interest levels wane.

No teacher would open with, "This is going to be awful,"— although I did hear one very nervous public speaker start that way. We're much more subtle with our warnings. For example, "I was up late last night grading your papers—let me see if I can get my notes in order here," or the infamous, "This won't be on the test." I've also seen the light of interest go out of students' eyes in response to "I know this is rehash for most of you."

Beware of telling students, "This part will be complicated and difficult to understand." One poor listening habit is to avoid expository, technical, or challenging information (Nichols, 1987). If we warn students that material will be challenging, this may inspire them to put this poor listening habit into effect.

If you go into each lecture with the attitude that what you have to say is absolutely vital to every member of the class and that your presentation of it will be outstanding (even if you *were* up late the night before), you'll create a positive self-fulfilling prophecy. Students' thoughts about classroom material will be positive, and therefore their action will be to listen.

Organize Effectively—
Help Your Students Follow Your Train of Thought

(Internal Noise: *"I'm confused; what's coming next?"* *"What was that point? I missed it."*)

Without good organization, a student can become confused by a lecture as quickly as a driver in a new city gets lost without a map. The "tell 'em method" ([a] Tell 'em what you're gonna tell 'em, [b] Tell 'em, [c] Tell 'em what you done told 'em) is the best safeguard I know of to keep students cued in to your lecture organization. In step one, give a preview of what will be covered during the lecture. Lay out your points in order. In step two, go back over your points, explaining, embellishing, providing examples, answering students' questions, and so forth. Step three provides a summary of what has been discussed.

As the speaker, the "tell 'em method" may seem repetitive. But for the listeners, the repetition acts as a map to help them know where the lecture has been and where it is going. While reading, if we catch ourselves daydreaming, we can go back and reread. In televised sports, we have the instant replay. If someone is talking during a movie video, we've got the rewind button. Listening, on the other hand, is a onetime experience. The use of repetition can help students stay on track and in the listening mode, even if they daydream for a moment.

Use Extemporaneous Oral Style—
Help Your Students Understand What You're Saying

(Internal Noise: *"This is too complex."* *"What in the world is he or she talking about?"*)

James Winans (Winans & Hudson, 1931) put it very succinctly when he wrote, "A speech is not merely an essay standing on its hind legs" (p. 17). There are distinct differences between language intended for the eye and language intended for the ear. In a study of the differences between oral and written language styles, Einhorn (1978) found that oral style uses many more personal references, more personal pronouns, shorter thought units, shorter words, more repetition of words, and words that are more familiar.

Written language presented in oral form is very difficult for listeners to follow. Therefore, it's best to stick with extemporaneous (speaking from an outline), rather than manuscript (speaking from a script), mode when delivering a lecture. This will help students to stay tuned in to what you are saying rather than concluding that it is too complex and tuning out.

Don't Let Your Words Cause Individuals in Your Classroom to Stop Listening

(Internal Noise: *"This teacher is biased. He or she can't teach me anything." "After class I'll give him/her a piece of my mind!"*)

There is a classic Abbott and Costello skit in which Costello is confronted with an elderly, bearded man who gets very upset at the mere mention of Niagara Falls. Try as he might to avoid mentioning "that place," Costello keeps getting roped into saying the words "Niagara Falls" and each time he does, the bearded man attacks him and beats him up. Something about those words greatly upsets that guy.

Most students in a classroom have words, phrases, or attitudes that really bug them. These are known as "triggers" and most often relate to issues around gender, race, cultural heritage, class, sexual preference, religion, political affiliation, age, and other similarly sensitive topics. When a teacher treads on one of these triggers, offended students stop listening on the spot and begin mentally preparing a rebuttal to the insensitive comment. This rebuttal may create a discussion (or argument!) during the class, a confrontation after class, or it may become a silent cause of alienation and poor listening for the remainder of the semester. This situation is known as "emotional deafness," and can be avoided (Wolvin & Coakley, 1996).

It is important to strive to keep our language free from bias and to be sensitive to the wide variety of diversity in our classrooms. Nevertheless, it is probably not possible to be aware of every student's trigger points. The authors of *Perceptive Listening* note, "It would be a boon to listeners everywhere if we could list the words that are the most emotion producing, and are therefore the most detrimental to listening. However, the list would be different for everyone" (Wolff, Marsnik, Tacey, & Nichols, 1983, p. 143). One solution is to communicate a receptive attitude that allows students to let you know if and when you've tripped a trigger. This can be as simple as saying something like, "I try to be aware of all of our various differences, and I always mean to be respectful of everyone in here, but if I say something that offends you, please speak to me about it."

If we increase our awareness *and* our receptivity, we'll reduce the chance that insensitive language in the classroom will cause the "Niagara Falls" syndrome.

Make the Most of Your Personal Communication Strengths

We all know that dynamism, humor, and sending chills down students' spines with dramatic stories are skills that make a professor a "good lecturer." But, did you know that simply deleting "um," "uh," and "you know" from your speech can increase your students' attention and improve their evaluation of you as a lecturer (Johnson, Vinson, Hackman, & Hardin, 1989)?

Everyone is good at some aspect of lecturing. Watching a videotape of one of your lectures or having a colleague sit in on your class and offer comments are both excellent ways to find out what you're good at. The feedback can also help you improve your lecturing skills. The elements that enhance a lecturer's effectiveness include clarity, logical organization, ability to pinpoint areas of confusion for students, knowledge of the material, enthusiasm for your subject, effective use of analogies and examples, effective use of extemporaneous oral style, rapport with students, use of demonstrations and visual aids, and interactive abilities. Become aware of what you're good at and make these qualities shine.

References

Barnes, D. (1992). *From communication to curriculum* (2nd ed.). Portsmouth, NH: Boynton/Cook.

Einhorn, L. (1978, Spring). Oral and written style: An examination of differences. *The Southern Speech Communication Journal, 43,* 302-311.

Johnson, C., Vinson, L., Hackman, M., & Hardin, T. (1989). The effects of an instructor's use of hesitation forms on student ratings of quality, recommendations to hire, and lecture listening. *Journal of the International Listening Association, 3,* 32-43.

Nichols, R. G. (1987, September). Listening is a 10-part skill. *Nation's Business, 75,* 40.

Winans, J. A., & Hudson, H. H. (1931). *A first course in public speaking.* New York: D. Appleton-Century.

Wolff, F. I., Marsnik, N. C., Tacey, W. S., & Nichols, R. G. (1983). *Perceptive listening.* New York: Holt, Rinehart & Winston.

Wolvin, A. D., & Coakley, C. G. (1996). *Listening* (5th ed.). Madison, WI: Brown & Benchmark.

4 | Lecturing 102: Using Stories and Examples

The lecture hall is packed, but the students are still and quiet as Professor Holly Shulman (History) reads, "When Dorothy stood in the doorway and looked around, she could see nothing but the great gray prairie on every side. Not a tree nor a house broke the broad sweep of flat country that reached the edge of the sky in all directions. The sun had baked the plowed land into a gray mass, with little cracks running through it. Even the grass was not green, for the sun had burned the tops of the long blades until they were the same gray color to be seen everywhere. Once the house had been painted, but the sun blistered the paint and the rains washed it away, and now the house was as dull and gray as everything else" (Baum, 1900, p. 1).

Is this a children's literature class? Agronomy 101? No. It's History 157 and Shulman is reading from the beginning of L. Frank Baum's *The Wonderful Wizard of Oz* in order to introduce the populist movement in the United States during the late 19th century. "Baum wrote *The Wizard of Oz* as a populist parable," she tells the class. "The tin woodsman represents the American industrial worker, and the scarecrow represents the farmer."

Storytelling is one of our oldest, most basic methods of communication and the transmission of knowledge about our world. As Nobel prize winning author Isaac Bashevis Singer (1984) once wrote, "When a day passes, it is no longer there. What remains of it? Nothing more than a story. If stories weren't told or books weren't written, man would live like the beasts, only for the day. Today we live, but by tomorrow today will be a story. The whole world, all human life, is one long story" (p. 173).

Stories make concepts vivid and clear by *illustrating* them rather than simply explaining them. Especially in large classes, where the teacher is more of a lecturer and less of a facilitator, stories can help lecture material come alive for students. They can help students to feel more personally connected to the subject matter because they bring the "known" (the down-to-earth language and images of a story) into relationship with the as yet "unknown" (the course material). Author Sally Davies put it succinctly: "Stories help us to learn, but more than that, they help us to *understand*" (personal communication, August 4, 1997).

There are many sources of stories to spice up your lectures: literature, as was illustrated above, as well as family stories, examples from the media, and personal experience.

Family Stories

David Grimsted (History) makes use of family stories to illustrate his material. During one of his lectures about the early immigrants to this country, he first gives the students the facts and figures: Many of the immigrants were quite poor. There was a high infant mortality rate. Their lives were difficult on isolated homestead farms where they lived far from such amenities as basic medical care. Then, he tells a story.

When his grandmother was a little girl, her family came from Sweden to live on a homestead in Minnesota. During their first winter there, her mother gave birth to a baby boy. Soon after that, her father left his wife and children to work at the lumber camps in order to earn money during the long Minnesota winter. The baby became sickly, and when he was just a couple of months old, he died. Alone and isolated, and with the ground too frozen to dig a grave, her mother did the only thing she could think of: She placed the corpse in a burlap bag and put it in the woodshed where it would remain frozen until spring. Grimsted's grandmother, then about five years old, remembered her terror each time she was required to perform her daily chore: going to the woodshed to gather wood. The story illustrates each of the elements Grimsted introduced in his lecture. The power of the story embeds these facts in students' memories.

Stories From the Media

An excellent way to keep students in large classes interested in classroom material is to add the elements of drama, humor, or both. The media can offer dramatic stories to illustrate your material. Mary Ella Randall (English, University of the District of Columbia) says that when she reaches the point in the semester when she is teaching *Macbeth,* she can usually be assured of finding a story in the current news that shows how ambition and power corrupt. She finds that this modern parallel to an old story helps students grasp the themes in *Macbeth.*

The media can also offer humor. Salah Negm (Accounting, University of Maryland University College) has combed the newspapers and other media for years and has amassed a collection of stories that relate to his subject material. Here are some examples from Negm's lecture on tax deductions, taken from a *Washington Post* article on questions people ask the IRS: One question came from a man whose swimming pool burned down. Apparently, sparks from his backyard barbecue ignited the plastic lining of the pool and ruined it. He wanted to know if it was allowable as a casualty loss. The IRS's answer: yes. The IRS, however, was unable to help the bigamist from Baltimore who complained that there was space for only one of his wives on his joint return (Raspberry, 1979).

My own lectures in the Speech Communication courses I teach are easily enlivened with stories from the press. For example, when I lecture on verbal communication and how easily it can be misunderstood and misconstrued, I quote from an article in *Time* magazine that describes how the Pepsi slogan "Come alive with Pepsi" failed miserably in Germany where it was translated, "Come alive out of the grave with Pepsi" (Rosenblatt, 1981). It fared even worse in China where it was translated, "Pepsi brings your ancestors back from the dead."

Personal Experience

Joan Mele-McCarthy (Hearing and Speech Sciences) uses stories from personal experience to put life into the concepts she presents. Her years of working as a clinician in the field have given her a rich resource to draw from. "Too often, students feel that all they are getting is theory," she says. "The stories put flesh on the theory."

Personal stories help students to feel as though they've gotten to know their instructor a bit as well. This helps to personalize the otherwise fairly impersonal environment of the large class.

Or, you can bring students into a story to make it their personal experience. Dick Racusen (Biology) begins the semester by talking about how *life* (the main topic of biology) is very close to *nonlife*. He invites students to participate in this story by holding their breath. As they begin to get dizzy and feel the warning signs of blacking out, the concept of the thin line between life and nonlife has been illustrated as well as explained.

Storytelling Tips

An activity I use to help my speech students become aware of how they can find stories to use in their speeches is this: We listen to about 20 students tell family stories. Family stories are about one to three minutes in length and may be about any generation in their families, including those who passed away before they were born. The stories may be humorous, suspenseful, or simply illustrate a family tradition. After hearing the stories, we take a list of the topics these 20 students have chosen to give their informative and persuasive speeches on, and like a game of mix and match we match the family stories to the topics. In other words, we decide which stories could best be used to illustrate the topics of the speeches. Obviously, most students would end up telling someone else's family story, but they can always use the preface, "A friend of mine told me."

To use this method to choose stories for your lectures, simply make a list of your favorite stories, family, personal, from the media, or from any other source and brainstorm ways they could be used to illustrate the points in your lectures. You probably already have a collection of stories waiting to be told.

Racusen offers guidelines for effective storytelling in the classroom. "Humans like intrigue and gossip, tales of heroism and villainy, humble ideas toppling arrogant ones, and the like." The story of biology itself is an epic tragedy, he says; 95% of all creatures that have ever been on the earth are now extinct. As he chooses a story to illustrate his Introductory Biology lectures he asks himself, Is the story provocative? Does it surprise me? Does it scare me?

Len Barron, creator and performer of the theater piece, *Walking Lightly. . . . A Portrait of Einstein* (Profile, 1994), says about the use of stories in college teaching, "Stories convey many lessons at once. They give a sense of history, they carry a creative tension in the anticipation one feels in wondering how they will turn out, and—like a good example—they almost always involve establishing a kind of problem set that invites intellectual engagement" (p. 11).

Whatever your subject material, good stories will make your lectures better. Newspapers, magazines, radio, television, the Net, family gatherings, novels, nonfiction books, work and life experience, children and grandparents all can provide a wealth of material for the classroom.

References

Baum, L. F. (1900). *The wonderful wizard of Oz*. New York: George M. Hill Co.
Profile. (1994). *The National Teaching & Learning Forum, 3*(5), 10-11.
Raspberry, W. (1979, April 16). Dreaming up deductions. *Washington Post*,
   p. A27.
Rosenblatt, R. (1981, March 30). Oops! How's that again? *Time, 117*, 85-86.
Singer, I. B. (1984). Naftali the storyteller & his horse, Sus (J. Singer, Trans.).
   In *Stories for children* (pp. 167-183). New York: Farrar/Straus/Giroux.
   (Reprinted from *Confrontation*)

5 | Using Demonstrations, Visual Aids, and Technology

Creativity may simply mean that there is no particular virtue in doing things the way they've always been done.

—*Rudolph Fletch*

John Clarke (1987) says of visual devices, "They break the tedious stream of words, words, words, allowing students to see what they are hearing . . . they break the pace of discourse, shift focus from the lecturer to the material, and help stem the erosion of interest that occurs when students are fixed to one spot for fifty minutes or more" (p. 57). Laurie McNeil (1995) of the University of North Carolina calls demonstrations, "Concrete handles for grabbing hold of . . . abstractions" (p. 4).

Demonstrations and Dramatic Devices

The room is big, the number of students is huge, the microphone and/or room acoustics make your voice big, and your demonstrations have to be *big* if anyone is going to appreciate them. In a large lecture hall, passing around a moon rock or inviting students to view white blood cells under a microscope is not going to work. Demonstrations that are large in their appearance, their emotional appeal, or both will be the most effective.

In Lynne Greeley's Theater 110 class, two students move around the lecture platform performing a reader's theater of a section of *A Doll's House* by Henrick Ibsen. After several minutes of marital crisis between Nora and Torvald, Greeley interrupts them and addresses the class,

"Now let's change the given circumstances. What do you want them to do?"

"Move it up in time—the 1970s," someone calls.

"Move it from England to the United States," shouts another student.

"The South," someone chimes in.

The actors continue, with brand new accents and new ways of walking and relating.

Greeley interrupts several more times with questions. "How can Nora be more aggressive?" she asks.

"Stand up!" a student answers.

When the reader's theater has finished, Greeley engages the class in a lively discussion, moving among the students, shooting out questions and pointing at answers. Then, quickly, a screen the size of Rhode Island lowers into the room, the lights are dimmed, and we watch Jane Fonda and a costar act out the same scene we've just been talking about. The discussion continues during the film, with Greeley's voice piercing both the darkness and students' tendency to fall asleep when the lights are out.

It may come as no surprise that Greeley uses "dramatic devices." She is, after all, teaching theater. But, the use of drama in the classroom need not be limited to theater classes.

Grace Deming (Astronomy) makes good use of the 15,000 Physics and Astronomy demonstrations available to her. It's Thursday and there's the usual hubbub before class starts in Astronomy 101. Students discuss the "sky watch" from the night before (Venus and Saturn were close to each other in the southwestern sky just after sunset). No one seems to pay much attention to the man on a ladder carefully hanging a black 40-pound weight from a long wire in the center of the lecture platform.

Class begins, and students are attentive as Deming presents the basics of the scientific method: observation, hypothesis, experimentation, revision, and more observation. She explains how a well-supported hypothesis is sometimes referred to as a law, such as the law of gravity. She assures us that laws demonstrate consistency. She then declares that she will show her faith in the law of gravity, which dictates that a pendulum will not swing higher than its starting position. She grabs the 40-pound weight and backs herself against a makeshift plywood wall, which will prevent her from flinching out of the way. She holds the heavy metal plate to her forehead, and amid nervous fluttering among the students she lets go. As the weight swings out and away, there are tiny cries of "aaah!" and "oh!" As the weight plummets back toward Deming's head, students gasp. Deming, unflustered, uses this teachable moment to its fullest, "You see, good theories have repeatable results," she says as the plate barely misses her head and swings away.

Physics demonstrations are available from a number of universities over the Net. Those available from the University of Maryland include a photo of the demonstration, a description, and an explanation of equipment needed and how to set it up. They may be accessed on the Web at http://www.physics.umd. edu/deptinfo/facilities/lecdem/

Visual Aids

In a large class, visual aids will need to be impressive enough to capture the attention of the students in the cheap seats. Bright colors, along with sheer size, will help to do this.

In another science lecture hall, Dick Racusen (Biology) stands on the platform with what looks like the better part of his home's heating system held high above his head: a long, . caterpillar-like segment of silver tubing decorated with of day-glow orange paint. The ends snake onto the floor around his feet. He's lecturing about protein structure. "This is what a scaled-up enzyme looks like," he explains, before he stuffs the oversized larva back into the large black trash bag that is its home.

Racusen says he often brings in a large black trash bag and sets it on the stage before the lecture begins. Students wait expectantly to find out what's in it. Some days they find out, and other days the bag simply serves to keep them alert and hoping, until he ends the lecture, picks up the bag, and leaves.

"These devices are better if they look like I thought of them at midnight last night," says Racusen. "That way, they look inspired." The well-developed, professional stuff is, he maintains, less interesting.

Uses of Technology

When I was getting my Master's degree, a fellow student gave a presentation on the use of visual aids. I remember he spent a lot of time talking about which color magic markers to use on newsprint. Last week I met with Dr. Richard Berg of the Physics Department to discuss visual aids. He showed me how to bring up the latest NASA photographs of comet Hyakutake by downloading them from the Net and then projecting them on the big screen using a liquid crystal control panel at the podium.

In the past decade, there have been huge increases in the possibilities for visual aids and technology in the classroom. It's not always easy to keep up with all of the opportunities, and for many faculty, learning to use the new technologies seems daunting. Next, we'll look at some of the tried-and-true kinds of visual aids, such as overheads and videos. We'll also discuss some of the newer forms of visuals, such as the use of presentation software to build a lecture and the use of the Net as a teaching tool.

Overheads

What's good about overheads? They keep students oriented to the lecture. They make clear the most important points to write down. They add a visual component to the aural experience of the lecture. On our initial questionnaire, students in large classes often commented that a lecture outline, whether in the form of handouts or on an overhead, was very much appreciated.

What are the disadvantages of overheads? If you turn the lights out in order to make them show up well, the darkness can tend to make students sleepy and can also reduce the visual component of the lecture, which is *you* walking around and speaking. A good solution is to keep some or all of the lights on. The overhead image will be fainter but still possible to read, and you'll have a bright room that is conducive to teacher-student interaction and alertness.

There also can be a tendency among students to only write down what is on the overhead and not add any of your details to their notes. It's a good idea to let them know, and remind them often, that what is on the screen is an outline and not meant to cover everything they'll need to grasp from the lecture.

Videos—Professionally Produced

There are many professionally produced videos available for classroom use. One important caution: preview the entire length of any video you plan to use in class. Just because the title and description sound as if they will fit perfectly with the unit you are teaching, this doesn't guarantee that the video will, in fact, be worth the class time it will take up. Although many videos are updated every few years by the companies that produce them, some are not. If the video is outdated, poorly done, or boring, it will fall flat. Or worse, an outdated video can be outright sexist (it's amazing how far the media has come on this issue in the past several years!) and you could end up discussing issues the video was never intended to bring up.

Another important point is to prepare students before the video is shown so that they will get the most out of the content. What major concepts should they be listening for? What concepts already covered in class will be illustrated by the video? A short lecture, a printed outline, or both can be excellent preparation for students.

Christine Fortin (French and Italian) often uses news programs and documentaries in French to help her students learn vocabulary and learn about French culture. In order to prepare them, she transcribes the text of the video and uses this to coach students on new vocabulary, new expressions, and elements of French culture. She also provides a written exercise for students to complete in class that uses the new words. Only after this preparation does Fortin show the video. She follows up with quizzes so that newly acquired vocabulary and knowledge is not lost.

Videos—Homemade

Sometimes it's not the slick, fast-paced, well-acted video that will be the most effective in supporting your classroom material. Joan Mele-McCarthy (Hearing & Speech Sciences) finds that homemade videos, the kind she tapes (with permission) during various sessions with clients, are the best for illustrating the speech disorders she lectures about in class.

Mele-McCarthy gives a lecture on craniofacial impairments that affect speech. She then shows a video of a little girl, Marina, from Russia. Marina has a cleft palate and cleft lip that were surgically repaired, but poorly. "See how she grimaces when she says the 's' sound?" Mele-McCarthy asks, pushing the pause button so students can get a good look. She emphasizes that seeing the "real thing" is what makes the concepts come alive for students. "They see that it's not just words in a book. This is what the words in the book *look like.*"

There are "unprofessional" parts of the tape, such as trying to get Marina to pay attention when she's more interested in the toy she's holding. "Marina, look at the camera." "I *am* looking." "Your head is looking but your eyes are not. Eyeballs, Marina." And we see Marina's chagrined look when she gives us her "eyeballs." These "mistakes" only serve to make the viewing experience more immediate. As one student commented, "It held my attention because it was real, kind of like home video, it was a real situation."

Do make sure to preview, edit, and carefully select your homemade tapes. Their "unprofessional" quality will need to be offset by their clear, immediate value as a learning tool.

The Net—Teaching Students to Use It

Although at most universities every student has an e-mail account and the dorm rooms are hard-wired, not all students have yet mastered the use of the Internet. If there are resources on the Net that would be valuable for your students to access, or if you have provided them with a web page, it can be helpful for you take some time during class to give students a hands-on tutorial on how to find their way through the menus to the items they'll need. Hook up a computer to the big screen and take them through the steps slowly enough so they have time to take notes. This is a situation in which, truly, a picture is worth a thousand words.

The Net as a Teaching Tool During Class

Sometimes those resources you want your students to be able to access on the Net are important enough to use as teaching tools during a lecture. For example, for a physics or astronomy class, the slides available from the NASA home page can provide excellent visual aids. It is important to do your surfing first, so you'll know exactly which screens will be the most valuable as supporting material and can move right to them. You'll also find out during you own surfing whether there are any graphics that will take an eternity to download, so you won't waste time during class waiting for an image that may never quite appear. If you find that an image will take a minute or so to download, you can work this into your lecture by having material to present as the image goes up on the screen.

Pictures and movies will be the most effective illustrations for lectures. Most web-site pages that contain writing have too much print and will be overwhelming rather than supportive to your lecture.

The Net as a Teaching Tool Outside of Class

Many faculty have set up web pages on the Net for their students to be able to access all sorts of information about the class. What can you put on a web page? The syllabus, topics to be covered, copies of old exams, a bibliography of supplementary texts, homework assignments, solutions to homework assignments (posted after the homework is due), lecture summaries, generic hints for problem solving, tips for doing well in the class. These items can be typed in or scanned in.

Guido Francescato (Architecture) would add one more item to the list of things you can put on a web page: graphics. He has scanned in images of buildings, plans, parks, and gardens that go along with his lectures. To the graphics he adds class notes so that students will be able to access the illustrations and explanations as a supplement to what they see and hear in class. For his classes of 500 students, Francescato hopes that this extra support will help students stay on track. He has received many unsolicited comments from students by e-mail saying that they use the Web site and that it is very helpful.

Francescato notes that when entering graphics on a web site, they will need to be manipulated. In order for students to be able to bring up an image quickly, it needs to be reduced by the number of kilobytes it uses up. Otherwise, the downloading process will be time-consuming and frustrating. He then works with cropping, resolution, and contrast to get the image to look right.

Electronic Tutorials

Textbook publishers have joined the technology revolution, and many now provide electronic tutorials to go along with the textbook. Spencer Benson (Biology) has gotten strong positive feedback from his students about his use of the tutorial during class. Before he brings it into class, he previews the entire tutorial so he can choose the parts that are most important. Then he brings in a laptop, hooks it up to the big screen and works through the selected parts while the students watch. The tutorial has some animation and some moving parts that add to the visual experience of the information.

Benson also has used the tutorial as an exercise in active learning. He invites students to come up and manipulate the laptop. If they get a question wrong, the computer won't let them continue. Students in the gallery then can lend their expertise until the right answer is found.

The disadvantage to the use of the tutorial, says Benson, is the amount of time it takes. About 20 minutes is a good amount of time to spend on it, but because the tutorial is a review of previously covered material from the viewpoint of the textbook, these are 20 minutes during which no new material is covered. Still, he plans to continue using this teaching method. When students were asked to indicate something they liked about the class, the tutorial was mentioned the most often.

Presentation Software for Lectures

Some textbook companies now provide CD ROMs with which it is possible to build a lecture with slides. Nevertheless, several of the faculty members I spoke with, who are using slides to support their lectures, preferred Power Point™ for Lectures as their software of choice. They find that an easy way to add graphics to the slides is to scan in photos from the textbook's CD ROM.

David Sicilia (History) builds his lectures with a combination of slides containing bullets covering key points and photographs. For example, in his lecture on the civil rights movement in this country, he discusses desegregation efforts after World War II. He tells us how Jackie Robinson was the first black admitted into the major leagues in 1948, and the next slide is a photograph of Jackie Robinson sliding into home plate.

Sicilia finds many advantages to building his lectures with presentation-maker software.

- There is no writing on the board. This saves time and prevents him from having to turn his back to the class periodically. (The time during which the professor turns his back to write on the board is a time when students can become distracted and begin to chat with each other.)

- The large type is much easier to see than writing on a board, and the color slides (for example, yellow print on a blue background) grab students' attention.

- Lines of type are added one at a time. Instead of a premade list of bullets, such as one would use on an overhead, the bullets are added to the screen as each point is covered. This keeps students from being overwhelmed by too much information at once and prevents the problem of students busily copying down a list of bullets while the professor is already discussing the first point.

- The slides keep the professor focused. In a survey course, which many large classes are, there is a lot of material to cover. This type of presentation imposes a discipline. It makes sure that the material gets covered and that proper emphasis is given to each topic. It helps prevent digression.

- It provides a baseline for note taking. Every student will write down what appears on the slide. It is helpful, however, to remind students to also fill in information under each bullet.

Sicilia asked his students what they thought of these lectures, and their response was very positive with comments like "very effective," "it helps all of our learning," and "it is a great step forward in teaching." He gives suggestions for teachers who would like to use this type of technology.

- Use about 10 to 15 slides of bullets per 50-minute lecture, interspersed with a few slides of photographs or other graphics. This should provide a comfortable pacing, with time to discuss each point and without overloading students with too many slides. Be sure to spend enough time talking about each slide so that students have time to write down what is on it.

- Don't try to design color schemes yourself. The software comes with templates with color schemes, and it is best to use these.

- Don't put too much on a screen. Keep the amount of writing concise. About five bullet points should be the maximum per screen.

- If you scan a photograph into your lecture from a source other than the textbook, keep a record of where you got it and adhere to fair use laws. (In other words, you are free to use the photo in class, but don't sell it in any form.)

- From time to time, turn on the lights and present part of the lecture in the traditional mode. This change gets students' attention and makes the overall presentation more effective.

Sicilia assures us that as you get used to building your lectures with presentation software it will become easier and less time consuming. It used to take him two hours to prepare a lecture, and with practice he has shortened that time to about 30 minutes. And your lectures can be archived, so they are there for you to modify and use again next semester.

Video clips also can be interspersed with the bullet slides or even spliced together with the bullets. Gina Marchetti (Comparative Literature) uses the technique of combining both words and a moving image on one screen in order to illustrate the concepts she presents in her Film, Form, and Culture class. This way, she can break the video down, start and stop it, and focus students' attention on minute aspects of the film, while having her main points show on the screen at the same time.

Marchetti also makes use of the "pencil" provided by the Power Point software. The pencil makes a slide become like a chalk board, so she can draw on the images. She controls the pencil with a mouse on her own screen. She can use the pencil to point things out, circle them, underline, draw arrows, or quickly write a bit of information and then erase it.

Marchetti finds that printing the slides and giving them out to her students helps students review what they have learned. Written information and still images appear on the printout.

The addition of multimedia visual aids can assist the learning process by illustrating concepts and providing information through both the visual and aural channels at once. It requires effort on the part of the instructor to first learn how to use the technology and then to incorporate the technology into a lecture, but those who are using multimedia in their classrooms feel it is well worth it.

Using E-Mail:
Problems and Solutions

E-mail can be a very efficient way to facilitate communication in large classes. It may be used to make announcements, answer student questions, or even have class discussions outside of class time.

Like any new teaching technique, e-mail has its glitches. Fortunately, there are others who have gone before us and learned where the glitches are and how to prevent them. During an e-mail brainstorming session, these avant-garde faculty shared their wisdom. Using e-mail with large classes, we found, has its own unique set of stumbling blocks. Next, you'll find some problems faculty have run into when first introducing e-mail as a teaching and communication tool in their large classes. Also provided are the solutions that were found to be the most effective in combating these problems.

Problem: Cheating. It's easy for a student to receive e-mail from someone, make minor modifications, and then hand the writing in as his or her own work.

Solution: There is a program that was written at MIT that can compare "cosmetic changes" and detect plagiarism. Telling students that this program is being used to screen all of their work has proven to be an effective way to curb plagiarism.

Problem: "Flaming," that is, students being rude and insulting to other students and/or using profanity.

Solution: Set strong guidelines about e-mail etiquette at the beginning of the semester. Make it clear to students that if they are rude, they will lose their points on that assignment.

Problem: Sexual harassment over e-mail, such as one student making suggestive comments to another student or TA.

Solution: Make it clear to students that e-mail is not anonymous. Calling the offending student into the office, printing out a paper copy of the e-mail harassment to show to him or her, and threatening to take away the student's account have all been effective in ending cases of sexual harassment.

Problem: Students who lend their ID number to a friend. The friend then proceeds to act irresponsibly over e-mail (insults, harassment, etc.).

Solution: As part of the class guidelines, let students know that they are personally responsible for everything that happens over their account, so if they give their ID number to a friend, they are still responsible for anything that appears on their account and will lose points accordingly.

Problem: Asking students for too much personal information, such as "write a short biographical account" as part of an assignment. This type of assignment can tempt students into flaming.

Solution: Keep the information on the listserv focused on class content rather than personal issues. If you do decide to use short biographical accounts as a way to personalize the class, set up strict guidelines about etiquette beforehand, as specified previously.

Problem: Busy signals! On many campuses, the number of people using e-mail often surpasses the connection capacity.

Solution: Avoid peak times (middle of the day Monday through Thursday).

Problem: Family members who pick up the phone while you're on e-mail and disconnect the computer.

Solution: No ice cream for that family member.

References

Clarke, J. H. (1987). Building a lecture that works. *College Teaching, 35*(2), 56-58.

McNeil, L. E. (1995). Challenges for teaching in introductory science classes: Why they aren't hearing what you think you are saying. *The National Teaching & Learning Forum, 4*(5), 4-7.

GETTING YOUR
STUDENTS INVOLVED

6 | Active Learning in a Large Class

"I don't have enough time to do active learning in my classes. I have too much material to cover."

"It's impossible to put my students into groups—the chairs in my lecture hall are bolted to the floor."

"My class is too big to use active learning. It would get too noisy."

"I've heard stories about failed attempts at active learning, and I don't have much experience with it. I don't want my class to fall apart."

"Students will think I don't know my material."

"Students will be resistant—they won't get involved."

"There's a long tradition of lecturing in science courses. I don't want senior faculty to think I'm belittling the way they did it."

The benefits of cooperative and collaborative learning methods have long been proclaimed, yet for many faculty members there is resistance to incorporating active learning strategies, especially in large classes. Neil Davidson, Professor of Curriculum and Instruction, and author of several books on active and cooperative learning, has found that using active learning in his large classes is just as important and just as effective as in his small classes. "If you want students to learn thinking, reasoning, problem solving, and decision-making skills, then it's essential to use cooperative and collaborative learning," says Davidson. "By actively engaging in the learning process, students very quickly develop new concepts, understandings, and skills that they don't develop just by sitting through the lecture."

What about the lack of time when there is so much material to cover? "There is always a conceptual confusion between coverage and learning," says Davidson. "The professor thinks that if he covered something, the students have learned it. If that were true, then everyone should get spectacular results from the lecture method." Davidson notes that social science research shows the adult attention span to be about 20 minutes at most and often much less. Combining segments of lecture with short active learning activities is an excellent way to keep students interested and involved. Naturally, improved levels of interest and attention increase learning. Thus, giving up a few minutes of lecture time for an active learning activity can actually increase the amount of information covered *and retained*, rather than decrease it.

Because a large class differs fundamentally from a small one, active learning methods need to be adjusted accordingly. Next, you'll find hints for planning, facilitating, and maintaining order during active learning in large classes. Each of the areas of resistance to active learning (in italics, at the beginning of this chapter) is addressed. Following this, you'll find a number of activities that have proved to be successful in large classes.

Running a Tight Ship
(With a Crew of 100 or More)

Planning: Be Prepared.
Make the Task Clear to Students

With your notes from last semester, you could probably manage to "wing it" if you had to do a lecture with very little preparation. Active learning activities, on the other hand, require careful planning and preparation. "Winging it" is often the cause of those scenarios you may have heard about in which the class falls apart and little learning is accomplished. First, decide on the purpose of the activity. What is it you want students to learn? Tailor the task specifically to the goal you want to achieve. Next, prepare the assignment in written form. Oral instructions are too ephemeral and can lead to confusion, especially with several students in each group interpreting these instructions. Rather than prepare 500 instruction sheets to hand out, an overhead or the blackboard (preprinted to save time) is usually the best way to spell out the assignment.

Make sure the task is clear, specific, and discrete. For example, "Create two multiple choice questions to cover this unit," "List the most important points you heard in today's lecture," "Come to a consensus about the answer to the following question . . .," or "List as many (fill in the blank) as you can in the next 4 minutes."

Anticipate student questions and be ready to answer them. In fact, it's best not to start until you've answered at least a few questions to make sure everyone is on the right track. (Allow several seconds of silent wait-time after asking, "Are there any questions?" in order to elicit queries.) Go over the instructions at least twice, and provide an example or two of an appropriate outcome to the task.

Ensuring Participation: Make Learning Objectives Clear and Require a Group Product

Many faculty members fear that students, especially in large classes, simply will not participate in group activities. Student resistance to these activities can be reduced if the purpose and learning goal is made clear to them, and if they are required to hand in evidence of their participation in the activity.

Either orally before each activity, or in writing (the syllabus is a good place to do this), make clear to students *what* they will be learning by participating in the small group exercises. Is the goal to improve their critical thinking and problem-solving skills? Increase their ability to synthesize the class content? Learn actual skills related to the field? Gain information? Practice communication skills, such as listening, speaking, cooperating? All of the above? Students will not view an activity as "busy work" if the objectives of that activity are made clear to them. And they won't think you're just killing time because you weren't prepared. Instead, they will understand that the activity is every bit as important to their mastery of the class content as is the lecture material.

Not all activities will lend themselves to a group product— something the group is required to hand in as evidence of the work they have done together—but it is a good idea to ask for a group product at least periodically. These may or may not be graded but should require students' names to encourage participation and attention to the assigned task and discourage students from simply using group time as "chat" time.

Maintaining Order:
Limits on Time and Group Size

In a small class, a group activity may be quite complex and take up a large portion of the class time. In a large class, it is usually best to keep group work fairly simple and the time frame short. These limits will help maintain both classroom order and your lecture's momentum. Most of the faculty I interviewed use time periods of from two to ten minutes for group activities, interspersed with segments of the lecture. They find that this format stimulates student interest, and provides an opportunity for student thinking, discussion, and learning. Nevertheless, the group activities are not depended on for large blocks of learning.

In small classes, groups of four or five students are considered optimum. But the bolted-down chairs and potential noise levels in large lecture halls make groups of this size unwieldy. Having students simply turn to the person next to them and pair up, or twist around to form triads, seem to be the most manageable ways to "group" in large classes. These smaller groups will help keep noise levels down and task completion may take less time because each group will have fewer opinions to contend with.

Methods

Below you'll find the blueprints for a number of active learning activities, all of which have been tested (and found to be successful!) in large classes.

Participatory Lecture

Peter Frederick (1987) suggests involving students in large lectures by asking them to contribute to the lecture. He calls this an interactive, or participatory lecture. If part of your lecture will consist of a list of things, why not have students begin the list for you by shouting out suggestions? Write their suggestions on the board or overhead, and then complete the list with anything they left out. Or, if you have a statement to make, pose it as a question instead, so that students can take part in making the statement.

Using a participatory lecture can be an excellent way to begin a unit or topic as well. Students are invited to shout out everything they know (or think they know) about the topic or issue you are about to cover. Their answers are written on the board or overhead, and then as your lecture progresses, their answers may be referred to as examples. This method is also a good way to find out just how much information, misinformation, or both your students have about a particular subject.

The participatory lecture also may be used to create mental or visual images to go with your lecture. Students are asked to think about a recent reading, laboratory experiment, demonstration, event, or experience. They then are asked to call out a brief description of the most salient image that has stuck in their minds from this reading, experience, etc. The mental collage of images that results will enhance the visual aspects of the topic you are covering, and make your lecture much more vivid.

As a break from the one-way lecture, the participatory lecture, Frederick (1987) says, "begins a jointly created coherent understanding of the topic" (p. 47).

Think-Pair-Share

Think-pair-share is a simple cooperative learning exercise. The instructor asks a question or poses a problem. Students spend a minute or two *thinking* about an answer or solution. Students then *pair* up to discuss (*share*) their answers. The instructor then may ask for several students to *share* their answers with the whole class. The method may be used with any subject matter, and need only take a few minutes of class time.

Spencer Benson (Biology) uses think-pair-share during most of his class sessions. Before the lecture, TAs quickly pass out "lecture ballots," which are preprinted half-sheets of paper with space for students to fill in their name and date, check off their discussion section, and then answer an as yet undisclosed question. As the lecture begins, students know they need to listen so that when the question is asked they'll be able to give an intelligent answer. About 15 to 20 minutes into the lecture, Benson puts the question or problem up on the overhead. For example, "Give three minimum basic requirements for life at a cellular level." Students have 40 to 60 seconds to think, one minute to write, and then a minute or two to talk about their answer with the person next to them. ("If you're sitting by yourself," Benson tells his students, "*move.*") He uses a beeping timer to signal the minutes. During the discussion time, Benson leaves the podium and walks around the lecture hall, eavesdropping on student conversations. When the discussion time is over, he picks students at random to either share their answer orally or to go down front and write their answer on the board. Their answers often spark further discussion. The ballots are collected and graded simply: one check for "Okay," two checks for "Good," three checks for "Great."

Benson has received a lot of positive feedback from students about this teaching method. Students appreciate the chance to come up with answers and solve problems themselves in order to test their level of understanding. Having a chance to talk with their neighbors helps to make the large class a little more personal, and the interruption of the lecture with an activity helps keep them awake and interested.

Benson also finds that this activity reveals how effective his lecture has been up to that point. If the first six groups he calls on have gotten a wrong answer, he knows he needs to review. If the first two or three get the right answer, he knows it's going well.

At Harvard University, Physics professor Eric Mazur, interviewed for a video (The President and Fellows of Harvard College, 1992) adds a twist to think-pair-share. During the *think* phase, students solve a physics problem, mark down their answer, and rate how confident they feel about the correctness of their answer. For the *pair* phase, Mazur gives students one minute to convince their neighbor of their answer. After discussing the problem with a classmate, students then give a revised answer that may be different from their first response, and again rate their confidence in their answer. Students' ballots have shown a dramatic increase in the confidence level of students on their second answer after they have had a chance to talk with their fellow students about the problem. They also show a dramatic increase in the percentage of correct answers.

Mazur (The President and Fellows of Harvard College, 1992) is strongly convinced of the value of this teaching method. After he began to implement active learning in his classes, he noticed a much higher level of attendance, his students were more alert than he had ever seen them before, and there was a major improvement in their understanding of the basic concepts covered in his course. One Harvard undergraduate commented, "I think that interactive learning can work in all courses. . . . You are doing the thinking—there is an 'Aha!' kind of sensation that, 'I figured it out!' It's not that someone just told it to me. I actually figured it out. And because I can figure it out now, that means I can figure it out on the exam, I can figure it out for the rest of my life. . . . It's not passive, it's *active* learning."

Student Demonstrations

"I would love some volunteers," says Frances Gulick at the start of her precalculus class. Hands go up immediately. "Who will do X squared? You will, good. Who will do square root of X for me? You, good." Students leave their seats and begin to line up at the board. Chalk squeaks as students busy themselves filling in the answers they are responsible for and laughing as they elbow each other for space at the board. There's chatting as the students in their seats compare their own answers with those appearing on the board.

"Who wants to be the incoming police chief?" asks Gayle Fisher-Stewart (Criminology). She chooses a volunteer from the upper tiers of her lecture hall and he runs down the aisle to join her in front of the class. As the class listens, she provides the new "chief" with the following scenario: "You pull over a car going 90 mph in a 45-mph zone. The driver opens the window, smiles, and says, 'Hello, son!' Are you going to give a ticket to your *mother?*" The student thinks. The class chuckles. Finally, the chief gives his answer. "Yes," he says. Fisher-Stewart commends the student on his correct answer, and notes that this was one of the questions the present police chief of Montgomery County had to answer during her interview. She also answered "yes," and got the job.

Student demonstrations can be a quick way to make a point more vivid, give students a chance to hear from their peers, and give everyone in the class a "think break." The volunteer police chief was not the only one mulling over what he would do if he caught his mother speeding. Each student in the room was asking himself or herself the same question (which is probably what resulted in all that chuckling). So, although only one or a handful of students may participate physically in the demonstration, the whole class has a chance to participate mentally. This enlivens the atmosphere in the lecture hall, and revives student interest and attention.

Games

Games can be a welcome break from lecturing and a chance to review class content in an entertaining way. Whereas in a small class all students can play, in a large class it is best to have a few students play while others watch. Joel Geske (1992) uses a question and answer game in his large classes, patterned loosely after Trivial Pursuit. Students are offered a few extra credit points if they volunteer to play and answer three out of four questions correctly. Usually, two or three students come up front and work together to decide on the correct answers. Students in the audience participate by calling out suggestions, clapping, groaning, and generally treating the short game session like interactive TV. The questions used may be typical of exam questions, and a few may be obscure, gleaned from sources like the *Guinness Book of World Records*. Questions from the text and lectures help review course content, and obscure questions add an element of fascination and, potentially, humor.

Departmental Support

Mitali Sen (Sociology) stresses the importance of departmental support in helping the faculty to incorporate active learning methods in their large classes. The faculty and TAs alike may be hesitant to adopt anything experimental and new. Training and peer sharing can help break through this hesitancy. It can be extremely enlightening and encouraging for the faculty and TAs to get together to share knowledge and resources, and discuss what types of active learning strategies they are using in their classes, what successes they've had and what kinds of difficulties have come up. More experienced faculty members may offer tips to those who are just beginning to incorporate new teaching methods. "If two or three people use [active learning]," says Sen, "you have a basis for legitimacy."

References

Frederick, P. J. (1987). Student involvement: Active learning in large classes. In M. Weimer (Ed.), *New directions for teaching and learning: Teaching large classes well* (pp. 45-56). San Francisco: Jossey-Bass.

Geske, J. (1992). Overcoming the drawbacks of the large lecture class. *College Teaching, 40*(4), 151-154.

The President and Fellows of Harvard College. (1992). *Thinking together: Collaborative learning in science* [Video]. Cambridge, MA: The Derek Bok Center for Teaching and Learning.

7 | Are There Any Questions?

The cutting edge of knowledge is not in the known but in the unknown, not in knowing but in questioning.

—R. Thompson
(1989, p. 61)

Curiosity is the cornerstone of learning. How can we help students become more curious so that they want to ask questions in order to explore their curiosity? How can we create a classroom atmosphere in which they feel free to ask their questions? How can we use questions to provoke critical thinking in students? What kinds of questioning techniques will spark a discussion in a large class and inspire students to listen to and become involved in the discussion?

The use of questions in large classes will, of course, work quite differently from the use of questions in small classes. If a substantive question is posed in oral form, only a small fraction of the students in a class will have a chance to answer. If questions are requested in written form, the reading of these may seem a monumental task. The following techniques work to minimize the disadvantages of the "largeness" of large classes and maximize student participation through posing and answering questions.

Helping Students Question
the Material (and Life)

Remember the Doonesbury cartoon in which the professor is lecturing and the students are busily scribbling down everything he says, even as the professor, in utter frustration with their lack of willingness to *think*, gives them increasingly outlandish and absurd information? Did you get students like those in your class this semester?

Students often come to class—especially a large class—with an attitude of "just give me the information that will be on the test so I can write it down." It is a challenge to get them to think, to wonder, to want to know more than you included in your lecture—in short, to get them to become *learners* rather than memorizers.

William Nickels (Business and Management) begins each semester by provoking students to question what they read, what they hear, what they assume to be true. "Companies advertise what they want to sell, and people buy what they see advertised, right?" he asks the 500 students in his Marketing class. Students nod and murmur their agreement. It's a simple, obvious statement they feel comfortable agreeing with without much thought. His next statement startles them. "Remember all those ads for Dr. Martens? How about the ones for guys wearing earrings? And have you seen all those commercials for students to switch from ten-speed bikes to mountain bikes?" In the silence that follows, you can almost hear their brains doing a double take. "Oh yeah, right. There were no ads for those things, but they sell like crazy." Nickels then continues to challenge students' ideas about marketing, advertising, buying, and culture. After a few of his lectures students will never view a Nike commercial the same way again.

Nickels uses the following statement, along with illustrations of its truthfulness, to help students develop a habit of questioning rather than blindly accepting information. "Almost everybody almost all the time is almost always wrong." He pulls out real-life scenarios, in which those who were trusted to be knowledgeable were actually going the wrong way, to bring home his point. For example, *The Cottage Physician*, published in 1902 and written by a consortium of "the best physicians and surgeons of modern practice," states the most advanced treatment for diabetes: wear flannel clothing, eat no vegetables, puke frequently, and take suppositories carved from bars of soap (Weingarten, 1994). The first edition of the *Merck Manual* contained over 100 treatments for gonorrhea—none of them effective (Rovner, 1993). In mid-1990 *The Wall Street Journal* surveyed 40 economists about their predictions of economic growth. Thirty-five of them said the economy would continue to grow for at least 12 more months. That was just before the big recession of 1990 to 1991 (Herman, 1993). This exercise in bashing the "experts" is designed to keep students thinking and questioning rather than simply taking down facts to regurgitate on an exam.

Helping Students Feel Free to Ask Questions

Many students would rather go outside to pick up their morning newspaper in their underwear than ask a question in front of several hundred of their peers. It is essential to communicate to students that their questions are *welcome*, in the hope that the bravest among them will engage in inquiry. Robyn Muncy (History) has several suggestions she has found helpful for encouraging students to ask questions:

- Tell them their questions are always appropriate. Remind them frequently that you welcome being asked about the class material.

- Respond to any and all questions as thoroughly as possible. This communicates that you appreciate their inquiry.

- Request the name of the student who asked the question, to show that you value his or her participation in the class.

Muncy suggests treating even a dumb question as "the most wonderful thing that has ever come my way, and thank goodness for it!" "You can always make something interesting out of even a 'bad' question," she says. "Let it take you in some interesting direction."

To help shy students ask questions, Muncy uses the "one-minute paper." During the last few moments of class, she has students take out a sheet of paper and jot down one of the main points from her lecture along with one question they still have about the lecture content. They hand these papers in as they leave. Muncy reads through them (they're short), chooses a few of the most appropriate or common questions, and begins the next class by answering several of these. She finds that this encourages more questions to come up during class. It also tells her how well students have been following her lectures.

Asking Questions to Provoke Critical Thinking in Students

When I was an undergraduate in the Speech Communication department, I began a speech with a question my teacher evaluated as "the best rhetorical question I have ever heard" (for the beginning of a speech). The question was, *Have you ever wondered what will happen to you after you die?* Of course everyone has wondered about that, so the question prompts listeners to think.

A question that elicits critical thinking in students will not have an easy answer. It will not be one for which you expect to hear a chorus of responses. Maybe one or two students will take a stab at it, or maybe you'll just throw it out as a rhetorical question for students to ponder. Maybe the question will be on the board as students enter the classroom, and the first few minutes of class will be spent with students searching for the answer.

Muncy likes to begin a lecture with a question that promotes critical thinking (for example, "Why is it that women have been the only group in U.S. history to oppose their own enfranchise-ment?"), allow time for a couple of students to pose possible answers, and then launch into her lecture that will, by its end, have answered the complex question. "This models how schol-ars work," she says. It helps students see how to approach their own essays: They'll need a question and an argument to sup-port their answer to that question.

David Webster (Business and Management) uses the time when students are arriving at his Business Statistics class to elicit critical thinking before his lecture. On the board is a question. It is based on information students learned during the last class, but it has a new twist, so it challenges students to go one step further than the last lecture took them. Calculators come out as students set to work individually on the problem. The earlier they get to class, the more time they have to work. When ample time has been allowed (for everyone who was on time), students are given the chance to volunteer and explain the solution they came up with. Webster listens to student responses, expounds on their answers, and uses this as a springboard from which to begin the day's lecture. He finds that this method gets students thinking right from the start. It helps them better understand the new material presented in the lecture and also makes excellent use of the time before class begins.

Wally Cordes and Jim Wisman (1995) also use this beginning-of-class questioning technique in their large Chemistry classes. In addition to the critical thinking aspect, they pinpoint several advantages of this method:

- It provides a useful segue into the day's lecture.

- It is a good assessment of long-term understanding. If the same questions were posed at the end of the previous class, they would be more of a test of short-term memory.

- Dedicated students can determine how effective their study time has been.

- Less-than-dedicated students get a pointed reminder that they are getting behind in class.

- If the professor walks around the classroom as students work, he or she can get a feel for how well students are understanding the concepts.

Questions for Discussion and Participation

Faculty members often complain that in large classes students show very little respect for each other and begin chatting as soon as a discussion threatens to commence. "I've never found a way to get them to listen to each other," says Muncy. But with a little ingenuity, she has found a way to have discussions in her large classes anyway. When a student asks a good question, she turns it back to the whole group. This way, the group is responding to the student's question but through her, the authority. Then, as students respond with their own ideas or further questions, Muncy repeats each student's comment, sometimes elaborating on it. Everything is funneled through her authority as the lecturer. "I used to try to hand over the power to the students, the way I do in my small classes," says Muncy, "but that didn't work." Maintaining control of the discussion and making sure all comments pass through the lecturer does work.

What about participation in large classes? Muncy finds that an excellent way to engage students is to ask several questions that lots of students can respond to at once. "What kind of information could a historian get from the documents in your wallet right now?" she asks. The answers come flying, "my birthday," "my height," "age," "marital status." Muncy suggests using this technique as part of any lecture and especially as a way to reenergize students when their listening seems to be slumping.

Frances Gulick (Math) sometimes creates almost an entire class from questions and student responses. It is helpful to begin the class with an active learning activity. The movement, talking, and laughter from this activity set the tone for students to respond freely to the questions she then begins to throw out at them. Sometimes the answer she is fishing for is simple, like "five units" or "parabola" or "yes." For these, she expects to hear all 200 voices, and for the most part she does. When there seems to be a lag from the back of the room, she marches up the aisle. "I'm hearing a lot from up here—what's happening back there? Are you guys with me?" "Yes" comes the chorus from the cheap seats.

Some of her questions are more complex, and only a handful of students may try to answer. Gulick repeats the correct answer to make sure everyone has heard it. What does she do when a student gives a wrong answer? "I don't think I'm going to go with that one," says Gulick good-naturedly, then repeats the question. The same student gives the correct answer, and Gulick enthusiastically confirms it.

The questions are shot out at a rate of about three or four a minute, with snatches of lecture in between, so there's no time for students to stop thinking and "veg out." Sometimes the answers are mumbled, not coherent, as 200 students murmur what they're thinking. But that's the point. It's a *thinking* session, not a sitting-back-and-absorbing session.

There are a couple of minutes left, and the class begins to make packing-up noises. Gulick glances at her watch. "I've still got two minutes left," she says, "so I've got a *question*."

References

Cordes, W., & Wisman, J. (1995, September/October). Use of "warm-up" questions to start a class. *Relative to Teaching*, p. 3.

Herman, T. (1993, January 22). How to profit from economists' mistakes. *Wall Street Journal*, p. A1.

Rovner, S. (1993, January 5). Merck's goal: Communicate [Healthtalk]. *Washington Post*, p. 18.

Thompson, R. (1989). Learning to question. In R. A. Neff & M. Weimer (Eds.), *Classroom communication: Collected readings for effective discussion and questioning* (pp. 61-66). Madison, WI: Magna.

Weingarten, G. (1994, September 25). If it quacks like a doc . . . *Washington Post*, pp. F1-F2.

IV

MANAGING YOUR LARGE CLASS

8 | Assessment and Feedback in Large Classes

At its best, assessment is not simply a way to label students with letter grades; it is part of the learning process. Sabrina Marschall (Faculty Development, University of Maryland, University College) says about assessment, "Don't think of it as a pronouncement that a portion of the class is lost (the Ds and the Fs) and another portion is in danger of being lost (the Cs). Think of it as a series of signs and road maps that tells the instructor where the students are and tells the students how to stay on course or get back on course."

Whether we're talking about faculty assessment of student progress or students offering feedback to faculty about their teaching, it all goes into a loop that provides opportunities for faculty and students to better understand their own teaching and learning and to make adjustments accordingly. For example, the instructor gives a quiz. The quiz is an assessment of the student's learning thus far. This allows the student to assess his or her own studying habits and to make changes if necessary. The results of the quiz (how well the class did) also assess how well the instructor conveyed the material. The instructor may, on the basis of these results, decide to adjust his or her teaching style, the rate at which material is being covered, and/or the style or scope of questions on the next quiz. The next quiz starts the feedback loop all over again.

Likewise, when an instructor asks students to assess the class, their comments not only provide feedback to the instructor but also offer the students time to reflect about their own educational goals in relation to the class. Which activities and assignments did I learn the most from in this class? What does this say about my learning style? What does this say about my interests and strengths as a student? What areas caused me difficulty? From this, a student may glean a clearer picture of his or her own learning strengths and weaknesses.

This circle, or feedback loop, is most effective when it is allowed to work frequently throughout the semester. In small classes, frequent assignments create a molehill of work for the instructor. In large classes, the fear is that frequent assignments will create a mountain of work. Nevertheless, if there are only two major tests, that is, the midterm and the final exam, with no smaller quizzes or assignments in between, then there will be only minimal opportunity for instructor and students to self-assess, adjust, and learn from past mistakes. Frequent, short, even ungraded assignments will keep the circle rotating, keep the feedback loop in action, and will provide optimal learning opportunities. Next, you will find ideas about how to provide effective feedback to students in large classes, how to provide frequent feedback without giving up the rest of your daily activities, and how to elicit input from students as a way to improve instruction.

Course Planning for Meaningful Assessment

Assessment is about finding out where we've arrived. Course planning is about deciding where it is we want to go. A good way to ensure that you and your students arrive where you want to go is to develop clear, specific course objectives, share them with students, and follow them when planning class sessions and when developing assignments and exams.

A course objective is a statement of what students should be able to do or know after participating in class sessions and completing the homework. Ory and Ryan (1993) suggested using Bloom's taxonomy of learning outcomes as a guide for developing objectives (Bloom et al., 1956). The taxonomy categorizes learning into a hierarchy of six levels, starting with the simple, such as knowledge and comprehension, and moving to the more complex, such as application, analysis, and synthesis. Most classes will have a variety of course objectives, some with simple learning goals and some with higher-level goals that ask for more sophisticated use of course material. Once you know what your course objectives are and where they fall on the hierarchy of learning, you can then aim your teaching, assignments, and student assessments at those goals.

Marschall stresses the importance of listing your course objectives in the syllabus. "This helps them know what you think is important," she says. "It also helps with pacing in the class, and it helps avoid misunderstandings if there is a complaint about grading because the objectives are *written*."

Exam Logistics

Lowman (1987) stresses that instructors should be present on exam days rather than delegating the chore of exam administration to TAs. Students appreciate having their instructor present and in charge on a day that will be, by nature, stressful for them.

In a small class, it's easy to hand back graded exams in the course of a few minutes. In a large class, even this simple task can become time consuming and cumbersome. Lowman suggests having TAs (or student volunteers) take stacks of alphabetized papers to different sections of the room. Students can be directed to the corner where their paper should be (A-G in this corner, H-K over here, etc.), and papers can be handed out efficiently.

What about missed exams? Again, this problem is multiplied in the large class, and 30 desperate phone calls the night before the exam can get annoying. Geske (1992) suggests making one exam optional and thus eliminating or at least minimizing the need for phone calls and makeup exams. He offers four exams and a final. Students are required to take four out of the five exams. If they must miss an exam for any reason, then they must take the final. Students may also choose to take the final and use that grade to replace a previous exam grade if they are unhappy with one of their first four grades. Geske finds that, in addition to eliminating most of the instructor's headaches from missed and makeup exams, this method also helps to reduce test anxiety for students. They know that if they do very poorly on one of the first four exams, they have a chance to improve their grade by taking the final.

Nancy Shapiro (English/College Park Scholars) suggests allowing students to "own a piece" of their exams. Ask them to come up with good exam questions and, as you are making up your exam, use some of the student-generated questions. This helps students feel connected to their own assessment process, says Shapiro.

In making up multiple choice exams, Ray Weil (Soil Science) avoids questions that ask for only simple memorization. Instead, he focuses on "questions that make the student think or use tools in a slightly different way than in homework or class examples." "To me," says Weil, "it is this ability to translate the information and apply it to a new situation that is a mark of learning. Just plugging in the numbers or rattling off a list is not."

Excellent multiple-choice questions that cause students to think are time consuming to produce, and coming up with scores of brand new ones each semester (in order to prevent cheating) is a daunting task. Weil has found a solution. He posts a carefully explained and annotated answer key in a locked showcase for students to view, but he does not pass back the exam itself. In addition to allowing him to use questions over again, Weil says, "This allows me to build on previous years' exams without turning them into memorization exercises."

Frequent Feedback Without
Frequent Headaches

When Gayle Fisher-Stewart first began teaching the large lecture introductory course in Criminal Justice, the course was set up with a final exam worth 50% of the grade and only a handful of other opportunities for student assessment. After the first semester, she decided this did not fairly assess her students' learning. She felt as though multiple-choice questions (those on the final exam) were weighted too strongly in determining students' grades and that not enough opportunity existed for students to show their learning in ways that showed more depth of understanding. She developed a syllabus that includes much more frequent assessment: three exams, nine written homework assignments, seven in-class written assignments, and 12 write-ups of discussion questions from text chapters. She feels that this frequent assessment much more fairly helps students show what they have learned and also greatly contributes to their learning process. The in-class writing assignments, given by surprise at the end of seven different class sessions and covering the material from that session, keeps students listening and taking good notes throughout *every* lecture, just in case.

But, you may be wondering, how is it possible to give these many assignments, or even half as many, and still manage to have a life outside of grading papers? It is possible, by making use of TAs, by keeping the grading system simple for short assignments, and by requiring papers to be in a format that is easy to read.

First of all, TAs can play a major part in reading and grading homework assignments, especially when there is little subjective grading involved, such as the answers to questions in the textbook. If an assignment requires more subjective input from the grader, it may be helpful to work with TAs in order to ensure consistency of grading. Fisher-Stewart gives grading guidelines to her TAs and reads one section of papers herself. It also can be helpful to grade a few papers with TAs and discuss the rationale before sending them off to complete the grading themselves.

Rather than using a letter grade system for these short assignments, using a point system can make grading a simpler task. Many of Fisher-Stewart's papers are worth five points with a specific piece of information required for each point. Very brief assignments may be graded on a two-point system: two points for the right answer, one point for a partial answer, and zero for not showing up for class or "no clue." Short assignments also may be ungraded, in that a student gets credit for completing the work, but it is not formally evaluated.

Deborah Moore (Office of Continuous Quality Improvement) suggests periodically asking for students' anonymous responses to a lecture (What was the main point of today's lecture? What is one area you are still confused about?). These informal, ungraded written assignments help the instructor determine how well the material is getting across. The responses should be summarized for the next class, says Moore, so that students can get an idea of how their level of understanding (or confusion) compares with that of their peers.

In-class writing assignments, which require you or your TAs to read students' handwriting, should be kept brief. Often, one or two sentences can tell you a lot about where students are in their learning and where they may still be confused by the material. Students should be required to type and double space any assignments they prepare at home. You may want to require a minimum font size. An easy-to-read page requires much less time to assess than a sloppy one. Because of my own frustration with how long it was taking me to read sloppily typed student papers, I began requiring papers to be spell-checked and grammatically correct. My syllabus reads "when I get to the fifth typo, I will stop reading and hand the paper back to be retyped and the grade docked a letter grade." Since I instituted this policy, I have only *very* rarely had to hand a paper back, and I've been amazed at how much more quickly I can read through all those neatly typed, correctly spelled papers.

Feedback From Students

Traditionally, students fill out instructor and class evaluation forms on one of the last days of the semester and instructors get to read these long after the class is over. This system is not the best way to allow the feedback loop, discussed earlier, to function. To be able to get the most value from student input, ask them for it informally in the middle of the semester or even at the beginning.

Mary Allen (English, University of Maryland University College) asks her students to respond in written, bullet form to two questions on the first day of class: What do you like most about teachers? What do you dislike most about teachers? This exercise is not personal: they don't know her yet and she doesn't know their handwriting. Their responses help her to know how to better meet their needs and give her a feel for the personalities in the class. It also helps her students to feel that they've had input right from the beginning by expressing what is important to them. In addition, such statements as "I've had so many teachers who go off on a tangent and talk about their lives all period," can serve as a reminder to her of the kinds of things she should steer clear of in her teaching. The positive statements, such as, "I like it when teachers give printed outlines of their lectures," help her know what teaching techniques to emphasize.

Informal class assessments may be administered several times during the semester or once at midterm. You may ask such broader questions as "What activities and/or assignments have you learned the most from?" "Which have you learned the least from?" or more specific questions such as, "How is the pacing of lectures for note taking?" It is normally a good idea to include the catchall question of "Is there anything else you would like to comment on?" to make sure you've gotten all of the valuable ideas available from students. And don't forget to share a brief summary of responses with students. This will let them know that you value their input and will give them a sense of how their comments compare to the comments of their peers.

Assessment is not simply a method of labeling students with letter grades or labeling instructors as effective or not. It can and should be part of the learning in a classroom and should be designed to help students and instructors alike prepare for future learning and improvement.

References

Bloom, B. S. Engelhart, M.D., Furst, E. J., Hill, W. H., & Krathwohl, D. R. (1956). *Taxonomy of educational objectives: The classification of educational goals.* New York: David McKay.

Geske, J. (1992). Overcoming the drawbacks of the large lecture class. *College Teaching, 40*(4), 151-154.

Lowman, J. (1987). Giving students feedback. In M. Weimer (Ed.), *New directions for teaching and learning: Teaching large classes well* (pp. 71-83). San Francisco: Jossey-Bass.

Ory, J. C., & Ryan, K. E. (1993). *Tips for improving testing and grading.* Newbury Park, CA: Sage.

9 | Managing Student Behavior

Ignore them as they leave the room or chase after them and demand to know why they're cutting out early? Develop a foolproof method of taking daily attendance, or let students decide on their own attendance habits? Outlaw the student newspaper or figure if they're going to read it someplace, why not in the upper tiers of your lecture hall?

There are no cut-and-dried answers about how to manage a large class, but discussing the various methods of classroom management can prove very fruitful. In a brainstorming session held with UMCP faculty, we focused on the student behavior problems most often encountered in the large classroom and came up with some possible solutions.

The Problems

Faculty agreed on a number of elements of students' behavior that were considered the major problems in large classes. They were

- Side-talking during the lecture, especially in the back of the lecture hall
- Arriving late
- Leaving early
- Causing a commotion during the final few minutes of class by putting away papers and zipping backpacks
- Skipping class, except on exam days

- Side-talking during class discussions (lack of respect for what fellow students have to say)
- Reading the newspaper during the lecture

Underlying Problems and Solutions

Certain underlying problems were thought to be at least partial contributors to disruptive behavior.

One glaring underlying problem is a lack of respect for professors, for the class time, and for fellow students. Students in large classes behave in ways they never would in small classes. The physical space between the students and the professor seems to allow a sense of detachment and anonymity to set in, which makes students more willing to engage in rude behavior. Students also seem to attach little value to large classes. In other words, they conclude that if the University thought the class was really important, it would be taught in groups of 25 to 30. This perceived lack of value translates into treatment of the class time as not important. Increasing student-professor contact through personalizing the class (see Chapter 2), requesting and/or demanding respect through rules laid out at the beginning of the semester, and a discussion of the true value of the class, were all offered as solutions to this kind of problem.

At many universities files of class notes are made available to students for a fee. This makes it difficult to require attendance. In addition, the availability of these materials sends a mixed message about the importance of attending class. The faculty need to communicate to students that though they may be able to pass lower-level classes using these resources, they will be handicapping themselves if they don't attend class. If they simply use the printed materials they will not be learning to listen, to take good notes, and to synthesize information. If they have not developed these skills by the time they get to the upper-level classes, they may well not survive academically.

Different Strokes

I interviewed three UMCP faculty members who use widely different control styles in their classrooms. Their methods are as different as the opinions they expressed about why their particular methods were chosen. The important thing to note is that, for each of them, their styles *work*, and they are happy with the way students are behaving and learning in their classes.

The Classroom:
Sacred Temple of Learning

Dick Racusen (Biology) does not tolerate latecomers, side-talking, newspapers, or early dashes for the door. He does, however, expect less than perfect attendance.

At the beginning of the semester Racusen lays down the rules, ensconced in symbolism. The classroom, he says, is the Temple Of Learning. Outside in the foyer, where there are benches to lounge on, a soda machine, and ruffled copies of the student newspaper, is the Pagan Plaza. In the Pagan Plaza, students may do whatever they want. If they choose to enter the Temple Of Learning they must be prepared to act in ways that are appropriate or face the consequences. The consequences for inappropriate behavior are embarrassment and humiliation over the microphone in front of everyone. For example, this drama unfolded recently: A student sat in an upper tier of the lecture hall peacefully reading a newspaper. Racusen left the podium in midlecture, marched to the back of the hall and confronted the student. "Out you go," he said, simply and directly. The contrite student put the newspaper away, to which Racusen responded, "Leave or stay, but you won't read the newspaper in here." There has not been a single newspaper sighting since.

Racusen tells students that if they will be late or have to leave class early for some reason, they should not come at all. What, then, of lowered attendance? He says if they opt not to come to class, then they are subsidizing the other students and paying for a seat for a bookbag or coat. "It's like the airlines," he says. "If you have the kind of money where you can afford to buy a seat and then let someone else use it, be my guest." "There is a large silent majority who will tolerate a lot of unfortunate behavior if it is allowed to go on," says Racusen. "As an instructor I'm not afraid to act as a policeman and squash that type of behavior."

Laissez-Faire

The style that works for Herman Ammon (Chemistry) is best described as laissez-faire. "I have a very relaxed attitude toward attendance," he says. "They're paying for it, they're grown-ups. They can come if they want to." It's okay with him if students read the newspaper, and he doesn't mind some talking, especially if these things go on in the back of the room. The students in the front half of the room are generally more attentive anyway, so the inattentive behavior in the back can be tuned out. He has noticed that when he turns his back to the class in order to erase the board, the noise level normally goes up, but then it quiets back down when he starts to lecture again.

"If you constantly berate students about talking, this destroys the comfortable classroom atmosphere," says Ammon. For him, the relaxed atmosphere is more important than strict adherence to behavioral codes.

In Between

Mady Segal (Sociology) expects respectful behavior from her students but has also provided for the times when they will break her rules of classroom etiquette. Leaving early or arriving late to her classes is not acceptable, unless a student receives permission to do so *in writing* before the date on which the infraction will occur. This way, class disruption is minimized because when a student gets up to leave, Segal says,

"Ronda spoke to me about leaving," and goes on with her lecture. Segal is very specific about excuses that are acceptable ("I have an exam right after this class on the other side of campus") and those that are not ("I have to pick up my boyfriend at the airport"). Permission slips require the student's name, date, time they are leaving early (or arriving late) and why. She approves the request or not, depending on the content of the note. If a student surprises her by coming in late or leaving early without having first obtained permission, he or she will need to speak to her as soon as possible and tell her what happened—and it better be good. (Acceptable excuses: "My other professor kept us overtime." "I felt like I was about to throw up.") Segal says she would rather students attend part of class than miss the whole thing because of extenuating circumstances.

When there is persistent side-talking, Segal chooses not to embarrass students during class but calls them up afterward to say, "Don't ever do that again in my class." Nevertheless, if she is lecturing and several students suddenly begin talking at once, she assumes it is probably in response to something she said that they didn't understand. She finds that students are reluctant to admit that they missed something and feel stupid raising their hand to say, "What did you just say?" so they ask the person next to them. In this situation, she repeats, with extra clarification, the information she just finished covering.

Segal informs her students of the philosophy behind her rules. "This is a group, and we have both collective and individual goals. I've set up these rules so that we can meet our individual goals without interfering with our group goals." She then goes on to explain how each of her requirements will minimize disruptions in the class and thus further the group goal of learning the material.

Of her students' reactions to her behavioral requirements, she says, "Several students have shared with me how much they appreciate the fact that I don't let people get away with things in class."

Conclusions

Classroom control style depends on the personality and goals of each instructor. The important thing is to be clear about your expectations from the start and to communicate your expectations to students. Biology major Inayet Sahin attended a faculty workshop concerning classroom management. After listening to the presentations, she said, "I'm a senior and I've been in large classes my whole college career. Up until today I never knew that leaving class early or coming in late would bother my professors. I just figured the room was so big they would hardly notice." If behavior such as side-talking and leaving early bothers you, let your students know. It's a good idea to print up your rules in your syllabus and then discuss them once or twice at the beginning of the semester.

More Solutions

In addition to the solutions offered in the three previous descriptions, our meeting and a survey of the research on classroom management provided the suggestions that now follow.

Side-Talking

Noise levels can be an annoying problem, particularly at the beginning of class. It can be a daunting task to get a room of 500 students to quiet down in order to start a lecture. Spencer Benson (Biology) suggests some possible methods for doing this. You could shout at students that class is about to begin, but this sets an unfortunate tone. You'll sound annoyed, and this action treats students like children and alienates them. You could just start talking, but this often doesn't work, especially if the noise levels are so high that no one can hear you. Benson says the most effective method he has found is to stand at the podium, look at the class, and raise his hand. This gesture lets students know that he is ready to start and that if they don't quiet down they will pay the price: He won't start and they won't get the material covered.

Side-talking once the lecture has started is disruptive to other students and aggravating to the instructor. Here are some suggestions (that have worked) about what to say to the offending students:

For after class, "When you were talking during my lecture, it had the effect of disrupting the class. You probably didn't realize you were being disruptive—I'm sure you wouldn't want to do that. I'd appreciate it very much if you don't do it again."

"Don't come back to class until you have spoken to me."

For during class, interrupt the chatting students with, "The people around you are giving you dirty looks. Are you aware of that?"

Other faculty members have found that nonverbal invasion of the space of students who are talking gets the message across to them. This way, it is not necessary to say anything, but the students change their behavior. If the offenders are sitting in the middle of a nailed-down row of seats, it may be difficult to get close enough to them, and another method may have to be used.

Arriving Late

Collect homework before the beginning of class, and close the homework box a minute or two after class begins.

Lock the doors.

Leaving Early

Collect homework at the end of class.

Ask that students who *must* leave early sit in the back of the lecture hall in order to minimize disruptions.

Commotion During the
Final Minutes of Class

It is important not to let the last few minutes of class begin to erode, says Benson. If your class is supposed to end at 10:50 and you give in to end-of-class commotion at 10:45 at the beginning of the semester, by the middle of the semester students will begin packing up at 10:30. Benson makes sure that he gives *no* signals that class is about to end (gathering notes, returning to the podium, unrolling shirt sleeves). If there are five minutes left, he announces that he is about to go over some very important material.

One faculty member from The Ohio State University suggests remarking (with a smile) "You have four more minutes for which you have paid, and I shall end promptly, so just wait to grab your backpacks" (Mountford & Richardson, 1988, p. 15). Using the last few minutes of class to give a preview of the next lecture has also been found to be effective against last minute commotion.

Skipping Class

Give "attendance quizzes." These are quizzes on the lecture content with easy answers for anyone who has been sitting in the lecture hall. If students are present, they will probably get five out of five points; if they are absent they receive a zero. The disadvantages of this method of attendance taking are that it takes time out of class without adding any new material, it gives the instructor or TAs extra work, and it increases the number of people who come to class just to take the attendance quiz and then disrupt the class by talking and reading the newspaper.

Passing around a sign-in sheet doesn't work because some students will simply sign for themselves and for their absent friends. The one effective method of daily attendance taking I have found comes from Howard Smead of the History Department. At the beginning of the semester, students are assigned to specific seats. He has his TAs draw up a diagram of the seats with students' names. It is then easy for his TAs to take attendance by finding the empty seats and recording the absent students. This method is highly effective once it is in place, says Smead, but it does create chaos on the day students are being assigned to their seats.

Segal believes it is important to keep a positive attitude toward the students who do attend, rather than being negative about the poor attendance habits of those who don't show up. Though a high level of attendance is one of her goals, there are days when there are many gaps in the gallery. She never says, "What happened? Where is everybody?" or "This class is getting smaller and smaller." Instead, she says, "Aha. The select few," and then she teaches to the students who are there.

Reading the Student Newspaper

Denny Gulick (Math) singles out the offending student and announces "You won't be able to find my lecture in the newspaper, no matter how hard you look." He finds that the humor, combined with public embarrassment, discourages newspaper reading for the remainder of the semester.

Final Thoughts

Faculty agreed that laying down rules early in the semester, both verbally and in writing in the syllabus, is paramount to creating the classroom atmosphere desired. Also, enforcing these rules strictly during the first few weeks of class will prevent erosion of classroom etiquette.

Peter Wolfe (Math) says that the whole problem with student behavior can be summed up in one word: immaturity. That is to be expected, because they are young. Part of our job, he says, is to give them some maturity by teaching them that they have to deal with the consequences of their actions. Whether your classroom control style leans toward authoritian, laissez-faire, or rests somewhere in between, it is important to let students know from the outset what it is you expect of them and then hold them to those expectations.

Reference

Mountford, R., & Richardson, B. (Eds.). (1988). *A sourcebook for large enrollment course instructors: Contributions from the literature and OSU faculty.* Columbus: The Ohio State University, Center for Teaching Excellence.

10 | Working Effectively With Teaching Assistants (TAs)

Guido Francescato (Architecture) received his first appointment as a teaching assistant in Argentina at the National University of Buenos Aires during the dictatorship of General Juan Perón. He and the other TAs expected to run the labs and help the professor. However, shortly before the semester began, the professor made a few comments that were deemed to be in opposition to the government, and he was thrown into prison. Because this was a public university, no one could admit that the professor was in jail. Instead, the TAs were told that this was *their* course and they'd better get themselves together and teach it.

When Francescato became a professor, teaching large classes and managing a group of TAs, he decided to give his TAs more help than he had received.

Producing "Good" TAs

Respondents to a questionnaire distributed in large classes at UMCP often expressed that a good TA could make the large class experience positive, whereas a poor TA usually made the experience negative. A similar questionnaire given to undergraduates at the University of Washington (Wulff, Nyquist, & Abbott, 1987) showed that students felt "TAs assisted or hindered their learning in large classes" (p. 24). Without a doubt, TAs play a vital role in the learning that takes place in large classes. With so much at stake, TA training should consist of more than the professor handing them the textbook and telling them which room to report to.

Before the Semester Begins: Focus on Expectations

Francescato holds a full day of orientation for his TAs (which, incidentally, includes a pool party at his house). They discuss the objectives of the course, assignments, course format, semester schedule, and grading, and learn what will be expected of them as TAs. Francescato provides his TAs with a detailed list, called the "Ten Commandments," which spells out their responsibilities. He had found that some problems arose simply because no one had told TAs what was expected of them. The list, which includes such dicta as "You must obtain an e-mail account and check your e-mail consistently" and "You shall not ask another TA to substitute for you . . . without my prior authorization," remedies that oversight.

Nyquist and Wulff (1996) suggest that TA orientation include information on any departmental or institutional policies and procedures that concern TAs. These may include policies on such issues as academic dishonesty or sexual harassment. All TAs also should be made aware of whom they should consult should a problem arise and what situations they should discuss with you before conferring with the chair of the department.

At UMCP the Math Department uses its presemester orientation to train TAs in how to communicate a concept so that students can understand it. Says Karen McLaren (Math), "There is a gap between being able to do the math and being able to teach someone else how to do it, and it is important to try to bridge this gap before the semester begins." For example, TAs are trained to use questions to help students come to their own conclusions rather than simply spoon-feeding them answers.

During the Semester:
Focus on Skills for Students *and* TAs

Marie Perinbam (History) says history, as a major, has a public relations problem. Students don't perceive history as a field that leads to high-powered business jobs, and not everyone wants to teach. In order to remedy this "image" problem, the department decided to market the history major according to the skills students develop. In other words, history majors gain certain skills that would be an asset in many areas of the work force: They can think analytically, write clear, lucid prose, master and analyze large masses of material, and speak extemporaneously and well.

In order to develop these skills in students most fully, Perinbam says, the department began to focus on *what* they were teaching and *how* they were teaching. They divided skills by course level. By the time students take the 400-level courses, they are expected to have developed a lot of control over how they think and how they speak.

Recognizing that TAs are on the front line in this goal of enhancing and elaborating students' skills for the marketplace, the department set about to expose TAs to the very best in teaching methods and pedagogy. With help from faculty from the Education Department, the department developed and presented a series of workshops. The workshops covered a wide variety of topics, from "How to Feel Confident in the Classroom" to "Hands-on Learning," from lecturing skills to assessment skills. The series also included a session on developing a teaching portfolio, which TAs found especially helpful as they themselves prepare for the marketplace. The department established a $500 teaching award with the stipulation that TAs wishing to qualify for the award were required to attend at least three of the workshops.

History TAs found the workshops very valuable. Ed Wehrle said, "The most important thing [about the series] was that it was an indication from the faculty that teaching is important, that innovative teaching is important, and that improvement is important." John Wood has found that the sessions on active and hands-on learning have been very beneficial. Learning how to use techniques like the "one-minute paper" and various group-work activities helped him improve his teaching. "Before this," said Wood, "you had no training at all and you'd usually revert back to lecturing. As avant-garde as you'd get was forming a circle for a discussion. The practical teaching tools have helped me feel like I have control in the class." Wood also appreciated the session on teaching portfolios. He said this workshop was like a gift from the department, to help him make himself more marketable in the work place.

Linda Sargent, another history TA, said the workshops helped her reflect on her philosophy of teaching, encouraged her to respect different learning styles within the classroom, and helped her become a more effective communicator with her students.

Teaching as a Team

Teaching assistants are in an interesting position at the university. They are peers of the faculty in their common involvement in teaching. As students themselves, they are also peers of the undergraduates. In addition, they are often closer in age to the undergraduates they teach than to the faculty with whom they work. It is important for the faculty to remember that TAs are apprentices who must be guided and encouraged to improve their skills.

Lois Vietri (Government and Politics) stresses that an important element in helping TAs do a good job is to *make the teaching a team project*. In other words, put the emphasis on the *teaching*, not on the *assistant*. First, communicate to the undergraduates that the course is being taught by a group rather than an individual. Second, just as with any team, work on ways to function smoothly while tackling the task of teaching. And third, provide for the cohesion of the group. Improved cohesion will improve the team's teaching effectiveness.

Below you'll find specific suggestions to help you meet the goal of working as a teaching team with your TAs.

Communicate to Students:
This Class Is Taught by a Team

A good way to give more than lip service to the team-teaching idea is to communicate it clearly to the undergraduate students. This way, TAs will feel more comfortable in claiming their posts as instructors. Some effective ways to communicate this are

- Plan a way for TAs to take part in the first lecture of the semester.
- On the syllabus, list the class "team," alphabetized with the professor's name included but not set apart.
- Tell the students about some of the behind-the-scenes meetings that are going on in order to make this a team-taught course.

The Task of Teaching:
Working as a Team

Why not let your TAs in on some of "your" work, such as developing the syllabus or writing exams? Why not ask them for input on your lectures, just as you may be offering them feedback on their sessions with students? True, it may take more time to develop materials as a group and offer each other feedback, but this will add greatly to the learning process for TAs and will most likely increase the quality of lectures and materials for both. Faculty members have found it helpful to

- Write the syllabus together.
- Require TAs to attend lectures.

- Meet with TAs immediately after lectures in order to get feedback from them.

- Meet weekly in order to go over lecture outlines, plan discussion section activities and discussion questions, talk about teaching strategies, and decide how best to do review and enhancement.

- For discussion sections: Assign each TA several weeks during the semester for which he or she will be responsible for developing a theme, an agenda, discussion questions, and teaching techniques, and for sharing this information with the other TAs at the weekly meeting.

- Make up exams together. (This helps TAs feel a sense of ownership of the content.)

- Grade exams together. (This also helps with consistency of grading.)

- Encourage TAs to take part in the large lecture—10 to 20 minutes is a good amount of time with which to start.

- Encourage TAs to observe one another's sections, give input to each other, and learn from each other.

- Observe TAs' classes and offer teaching advice. (It's important to let TAs know that these visits are offered as support rather than as a way to "check up" on them.)

Unity of the Group:
The Care and Feeding (Literally) of TAs

As we listened to faculty members who were providing excellent training and guidance for their TAs, we heard a recurring theme: food. Before semester potlucks, weekly lunches, pizza parties, and debriefing dinners all figured prominently in TA affairs. And no wonder: In any group that is responsible for a task, it is helpful for the group members to spend time together when *not* working on the task. Research shows that as a group grows in cohesiveness it will also grow in its ability to get the job done (Napier & Gershenfeld, 1985). So, don't feel like you're wasting time if you take your TAs out to dinner or try any of the other following suggestions:

- Have a social at your house at the beginning of the semester.
- Go out to lunch with each TA on an individual basis at least once during the semester.
- Hold weekly meetings over lunch or dinner, either at a restaurant or at your house (potluck). This way, the group can work on cohesion and task in the same session.
- Hold a three or four-hour debriefing over pizza and sodas at the end of the semester.
- As an end-of-semester celebration, attend High Tea at the Ritz Carleton (reservations required).

After the Semester Is Over:
Focus on Improvement

Nyquist and Wulff (1996) note, "Assessing how well teaching assistants (TAs) . . . fulfill their roles is one of the most important, yet most often slighted, parts of the supervisory process" (p. 104).

An end-of-semester interview can be a very effective way to help TAs understand where they stand in relation to your expectations of them. In what areas are they doing well? In what areas do they have room for improvement? What are your specific suggestions for improvement? Nyquist and Wulff (1996) strongly suggest that you put your assessment and suggestions in writing so TAs may review them at any time and continue to learn from them.

Andrew Wolvin (Speech Communication) offers feedback to his TAs through a variety of means during the semester: He observes their sections and offers suggestions, he conducts a midsemester evaluation in order to get written feedback from students, and he reviews the usual end-of-semester evaluation forms filled out by students. When it comes time for individual interviews with TAs at the end of the semester, Wolvin consults his notes from his classroom observations along with the two sets of student evaluations. The TAs are offered detailed feedback and suggestions about how to improve their teaching for the next semester.

The challenge in working with TAs is to treat them as colleagues, not just as students, while still being aware of their need for apprenticeship. They must be given authority and ownership in their own classes while still being given guidance and support.

References

Napier, R. W., & Gershenfeld, M. K. (1985). *Groups: Theory and experience* (3rd ed.). Boston: Houghton Mifflin.

Nyquist, J. D., & Wulff, D. H. (1996). *Working effectively with graduate assistants*. Thousand Oaks, CA: Sage.

Wulff, D. H., Nyquist, J. D., & Abbott, R. D. (1987). Students' perceptions of large classes. In M. Weimer (Ed.), *New directions for teaching and learning: Teaching large classes well* (pp. 17-30). San Francisco: Jossey-Bass.

INDEX

About the Author

Elisa Carbone is the coordinator of the Large Classes Project for the Center for Teaching Excellence at the University of Maryland. As part of this project she publishes the Large Classes Newsletter for UM faculty and TAs. She is a member of the Professional and Organizational Development Network in Higher Education (POD) and serves on the Diversity Commision for that organization. Since 1992 she has presented regularly at POD conferences.

Carbone is also a faculty member, freelance writer, and workshop leader. She teaches in the speech communication department at University of Maryland University College, where she has been nominated for the Excellence in Teaching Award. She is the author of five published and up-coming novels for young people. She conducts workshops nationwide on such instructional issues as active learning, lecturing skills and teaching large classes.